Reviewers' Co

This book covers absolutely every possible aspect of addiction. Indeed, this book is a veritable wealth of helpful and invaluable information on the subject, but more importantly, you will also read some incredibly sad, moving and honest stories, about everyday people, parents just like you and I, who have lived with and, in many instances, lost their children to the Addiction Monster – for them, there will never be a happy ending – as the author plainly puts it at the beginning of the book 'a parent should never outlive their child'.

—Tina Avon for Front Street Reviews

Remarkably intimate. This book takes you to the deepest depths of parents' souls who are dealing with their children being consumed by addictions. These parents know first hand the severity of addictions and how families can be ripped from the core because they lost the most precious thing in the world to drugs...their kids. The stories these parents offer are gut-wrenchingly honest and will make every parent blink back a tear while pondering the fact that drug addiction is real and can happen to anyone, anywhere at anytime.

—Amy "AJ" Crowell, MBA, Author of *Loved Back to Life*
Association of Persons Affected by Addictions

Slaying
The Addiction Monster

Slaying
The Addiction Monster

*An All-Inclusive Look at
Drug Addiction in America Today*

by Sheryl Letzgus McGinnis

First Edition, August 2008

10 9 8 7 6 5 4 3 2 1

Cover artwork courtesy of Amy Zofko
azofko@cfl.rr.com

Library of Congress data applied for

ISBN: 1-4392-0901-4

Also by Sheryl Letzgus McGinnis

I Am Your Disease (The Many Faces of Addiction)

Available at amazon.com, B&N.com, booklocker.com, And iamyourdisease.com

Also available as an e-book

The Addiction Monster and the Square Cat

Ezine Articles Expert Platinum Author

Read Sheryl McGinnis' articles on addiction at www. ezine.com

Slaying the Addiction Monster

He lurks everywhere — He's not only on the streets. He's in our schools, in our homes, in our medicine cabinets, on our home computers.

A book for parents and teens that encourages open and honest dialogue about the disease of addiction.

Read what other parents have gone through.

Read their words of advice.

Read what the experts say about how to raise a drug-free child.

Read what the important signs of drug use are. Most importantly, read this book with your child and discuss it.

Read interviews with leading researchers in drug addiction.

It's never too early to talk with your child about drugs, but it can be too late. Don't be in denial. The Addiction Monster depends on that!

STEROIDS – (some slang terms) Arnolds, Gym Candy, Pumpers, Stackers, Weight Trainers, Juice

One day I came home to find that a kid I knew had been found in the hallway, dead from a heroin overdose. He would not be the last. I had managed to steer clear of the drug scene. I never smoked marijuana, never got high, in fact never experimented with any drugs. And for a simple reason: my folks would have killed me.

- Colin L. Powell

TABLE OF CONTENTS

Section 1

Section 2

To our two wonderful sons
Dale Ian McGinnis and
Scott Graeme McGinnis, RN

"Children make your life important." Erma Bombeck

From the beautiful poppy flower that gives us heroin to the home medicine cabinet and every place in between. Available 24/7

"The cruelest trick came from the Taliban, who allowed plenty of drugs and then banned music."
            Author unknown

Our beloved son, Scott Graeme McGinnis, RN, who lost his battle with the Addiction Monster on December 1st, 2002.

"What is deservedly suffered must be borne with calmness, but when the pain is unmerited, the grief is resistless."

Ovid, Roman poet

Forever 31

Forever 31
Is what you'll always be
For that's how old you were
When you left so suddenly

I know you didn't want to leave
Your dreams so full of hope
Now we are left to cry and grieve
And somehow try to cope

I'll never forget your loving ways
And that smile! And those eyes so brown
They will live with me for all my days
Lifting me up when I am down

Had I known when you were born
The pain your death would bring
Would I have borne you anyway?
I would not have changed a thing

I'm just so glad we had this time
And so sad that we had to part
But you'll live forever, oh son of mine
Deep within my heart.

Your loving mom and best friend

"Addiction is a highly complex brain disorder that will require a multi-pronged approach to treat. Drugs alone will not be the answer – successful treatment of drug addiction will require a combination of drugs and attention to social and psychological factors."

Professor Lawrence,
Howard Florey Institute, Melbourne, Victoria, Australia

ACKNOWLEDGEMENTS

There are so many people whose paths have crossed with mine since first I undertook the daunting task of writing my book, *I Am Your Disease (The Many Faces of Addiction)* that it is impossible to thank them all in this brief space.

I must take the time here in this new book, to recognize the people who have helped make *I Am Your Disease* so successful.

Many are people who have been gracious and kind enough to email me letting me know how much they enjoyed the book, if *enjoyed* is the proper word to use when writing a book about tragedies.

There are many people I don't know personally who took the time to write outstanding reviews of the book on major bookselling sites and other sites.

Some people have actually phoned me to tell me how much the book has helped them to understand that addiction is a brain disease.

My co-author on *I Am Your Disease (The Many Faces of Addiction)*, Heiko Ganzer, LCSW-R, CASAC,CH of Phoenix Psychotherapy, graciously allowed me to use his narrative I Am Your Disease by the Anonymous Addict as the basis for the book. I thank him immensely for that and for giving me permission to use I Am Your Disease for my website. Heiko contributed Part Two to the book on gambling, an addiction which is growing steadily among our youth! This shocked me. I learned so much from him. Heiko has again contributed to this book with his chapter on Enabling.

Larry G, of the Prescription Addiction Radio Show on WGUL in Tampa, Florida, (860 AM) lists me as a Friend of the Show on his website. The truth be known, Larry is more of a friend to me than I could ever possibly be to him. His glowing remarks about the book fill me with joy and gratitude and yes, a bit of pride. I am proud to be counted as a Friend of the Show and a new friend of Larry's.

A special thank you to Eric Nestler, MD, Ph.D., Amelia M. Arria, Ph.D., and Florida State Representative Aaron Bean, all of whom gave of their time and expertise to help me in this task of shedding light on the disease of addiction. I thank Claudia Black, Ph.D., for allowing me to include her work on alcohol and addiction.

A special thank you to Amy Zofko of a2z Designs who is not just my book designer, but a special friend who not only designed the cover for I Am Your Disease, but who has outdone herself again with her incredible design for this book. She worked tirelessly to bring it all together for me. If I could pay her for what her services are worth, she'd be quite wealthy.

I want to thank Billie Johnson of Oak Tree Press for her patient efforts in helping me put this book together into a cohesive form. The book would still just be saved in my computer were it not for her. I appreciate all her hard work.

I owe an enormous debt of gratitude to my husband Jack, for his invaluable input in this book, for all of his help and support and insightful advice. His many years of teaching 8th and 9th grade students have given him as much expertise in dealing with children as any child psychologist. I thank him for being a wonderful father above all. I thank him for all his love, and wise counsel, and moral guidance for our children, for his patience and understanding, for never being too busy to be involved in their lives, for reading to them every night before bedtime, for being the absolute best father any boy could ask for and for loving their mother wholeheartedly.

Lastly, and if not most importantly, I must thank everyone who has contributed to this book. These friends and soul mates have delved deep into their broken hearts to offer words of advice hope and comfort to others who may be just beginning this long, painful journey or who have been living the nightmare suffering silently.

Addiction is the Silent Disease; the disease that nobody wants to talk about. Nobody wants to acknowledge. It is the unacceptable disease. For acknowledging that you have addiction in your family is akin to admitting that somehow you have failed as a human being or a parent. Society looks askance at the addicted person and their family.

It's time to bring addiction out of the closet and to recognize it, confront it head on, and destroy it. As long as people are ashamed to admit that they themselves, or their child or any member of their family or circle of friends suffers from addiction, then the stigma will remain and many people will be reluctant to seek help in the face of such perceived castigation by society.

The people in this book have decided to throw caution to the wind, and reach out to help their fellow human beings. Their motives are pure and altruistic. I cannot thank them enough for caring so much for others that they are willing to risk the slings and arrows of others who might not understand addiction.

Not everyone feels comfortable telling their story publicly, however, and I respect that. With that in mind, I must thank a very dear friend, who, although not yet able to go public with her child's story, has been a true inspiration to me, prodding me along like a little mother hen, and sometimes like a drill sergeant, offering solicited and unsolicited advice, and in each instance, valuable advice. She has been an unsung hero and an unpaid one unfortunately, finding names and addresses for me, finding lost emails that contained important information, emailing people tirelessly on my behalf and offering brilliant suggestions. She has been the perfect Personal Assistant. Thank you *Linda – you know who you are!

Thank you to everyone who has helped me, who has inspired me to continue writing about addiction and thank you to all who will take the time to read this book. You make my heart glad.

When a life is at stake and it's your child, you become fearless in a lot of ways. I mean, you just become fanatic. Nothing ever gets done unless it's by a fanatic."

Martin Sheen (www.eonline.com)

Preface

Dear Reader,

This book is written from the heart. It is not intended to be a scholarly piece nor is its focus on the cold, hard statistics. We've included many statistics sprinkled throughout the book but primarily the book is about real people and real feelings.

We've touched on some of the most commonly abused drugs. For complete information on all drugs please check with your local library or government websites.

This book is filled with love and hope and sincere, heartfelt advice from parents who have experienced the worst imaginable loss; the loss of their precious child. Compounding the loss is that our children died of an "unacceptable" disease, that of drug addiction. There is no greater loss than that of a child. As profoundly heartbreaking as it is to lose a parent, it is still the natural order of things. Our parents are supposed to die before us. No parent wants to outlive their child. It is the cruelest of the cruel.

Some of the book will be hard to read, perhaps compelling you to put the book down, step back, take a deep breath and regroup before you venture on. But we urge you to see it through, and take from it what you need.

It's important to understand that Good Kids Do Drugs Too; Kids from the right side of the tracks who get derailed by drugs. Kids make mistakes. We don't believe that any of them purposely indulge in drugs with the idea that they will one day become addicted. If they knew the horrors that awaited them and their families, surely they would not choose this path.

But as stated in my first book, children don't look at the long term. They truly believe they're invincible, that they are in control of their lives and if things get too bad, they'll just stop. Would that it were that easy!

If only they knew, if only they truly knew what lay in store for them when they cross the line into the world of drugs, they might think twice. This is why it's important to sit down with your child and read this book together.

This is the perfect time to begin an ongoing discussion about drugs including everything from nicotine to heroin and crack cocaine, Oxy-Contin to crystal meth, to steroids, to "huffing" and everything in between. It is the perfect time to Listen To Your Child. Listen for the true meaning of what he/she is saying under the innocent sounding words and questions. Let the dialogue begin!

On the following pages you'll find advice, opinions, and suggestions from people who are opening their hearts to you, whose driving force in life now is to do what they can to prevent others from walking in their footsteps. I must amend this to "our" footsteps because sadly my husband and I are one of these parents too.

In these pages you will find information from NIDA (the National Institute On Drug Abuse) and also information from the DEA. You'll find websites where you can find the cold, hard statistics of drug abuse so we won't list all of them here.

There are also special interviews included – Representative Aaron Bean from the state of Florida, Eric Nestler, MD, Ph.D, leading cocaine researcher, Amelia M. Arria, Ph.D., Deputy Director of Research Center For Substance Abuse Research (CESAR) University of Maryland College Park, Larry Golbum, R.Ph., MBA, host of the Prescription Addiction Radio Show, Claudia Black, MSW, Ph.D., and Heiko Ganzer, LCSW-R, CASAC, CH. Our sincere thanks to them for so graciously sharing their expertise and opinions on the disease of addiction.

You'll read the words of our deceased children as recalled by loving parents; children who are speaking out from the grave about how drugs ruined, and then ended their lives.

We've discovered that one of the main hindrances to recovery is denial, and not just denial by the addicted person; but denial by the parents who find it hard to believe that their child could possibly be involved with drugs, and denial by the parents that they themselves are addicted.

The "not in my family" parents and the "had they been raised better, they would not have turned to drugs" parents would be well served to read what other parents have to say about addiction. Many of us were also in denial. Who wants to believe that their beloved child has turned the corner and walked down that dark street that leads to a living hell…or worse, to death?

At the end of the book is a very important chapter. It's a place for both you and your child to sign a pledge. It's amazing how much more forceful the anti-drug message is when it's right there in front of you in black and white. Remember – Parents are the Anti-Drug!

Children can learn from this that their word is their bond. It can teach them integrity and principles and reinforce their commitment to sobriety.

We're not saying we have all the answers. Nobody does. What we, the parents in this book have, is experience and newfound knowledge of drugs and addiction. We want to share this with you, hoping against hope that you never join our ranks; that you never join this club that nobody wants to belong to, that of a bereaved parent. It's important to point out that not only do parents suffer, but grandparents, siblings, and other relatives and friends suffer as well.

If you have not lost a child to addiction but your child is addicted, please understand that we know what you're going through. Our hearts go out to you. We hope that our advice and that of the experts in their field, and our experiences will be of some comfort and help.

If you have suffered the unspeakable loss, however, we hope you will find words of comfort here, knowing that you're not alone in your grief. We all stand with our hands to your shoulders.

Lastly, we strongly urge you to keep the dialogue about drugs an ongoing part of your daily routine. Nothing is more important than talking to, listening to, and sharing information with your child about drug abuse. Children who feel comfortable talking to their parents about drugs are much less likely to do drugs.

Reinforce your child's self-esteem. Teach them to believe in themselves and to stand up for what they know is right. Teach by example!

A word about the home situation when living with an addicted person: Your lives have changed now and everything seems to center around addiction, whether it is alcohol, drugs or gambling. Parents go through the motions, trying to get through each day without falling apart, scared to death they will lose their child. The child goes through the day wondering where they will get the money for their next score and at the same time experiencing feelings of remorse and guilt.

This is no way to live! Our advice is to try to maintain a sense of normalcy in the home, try to make the environment loving, and a place where your child will feel comfortable. Try not to walk around the house wearing sack cloth and ashes, spreading doom and gloom. Try to bring the joy back into the home even if only for a short time. Try to help your child remember the good times.

Finally, if your best efforts fail to prevent your child from trying drugs, then don't delay, get help immediately! The sooner a professional anti-drug program is implemented, (rehabs, AA, NA, GA, etc.) the better the chances for recovery. Try whatever approach works for your family, anything from the above groups to a holistic approach. There is no one way to deal with addiction.

Relapses are not failures. They show you the need to redouble your efforts. Addiction is a family disease. With all of you pulling together and giving it your all, the chances of beating the Monster improve greatly.

THE ADDICTION MONSTER

He came creeping into our lives, slowly, stealthily, insidiously, with no advance warning. No triumphal heraldry alerting us to his imminent arrival. No fanfare. No clues. Okay, well maybe there were some subtle clues but we were too busy with our perfect little lives to pay much notice to them.

He counted on that! He thrives on secrecy and subterfuge. He knew that if he alerted us to his presence we would call on all our resources and strengths to defeat him, to slay him, to banish him from our lives and yes, from the very earth where he lives and thrives, and grows more menacing and powerful with each passing day. He counts on society's lackadaisical attitude toward him, believing that he cannot sneak into their homes. He depends on us ignoring his presence or believing that he lives on the other side of the tracks, surely not in our ideal communities.

He knew we would divest ourselves of every penny we had to expose him, to cripple him and kill him, that we would do anything within our power to stop his onslaught. He attacks the most vulnerable of our society: our children. He preys on them, luring them into his grasp with promises of ecstasy and escape from their humdrum lives, while parents go blithely about their daily routine, unaware of the chaos, heartbreak and destruction of the family unit that awaits them.

He is the most hideous of all monsters, yet he exhibits no external evidence of his cruelty, no demonic horns on his head, no red flashing eyes, no mien any different from anyone else's in the communities where he plies his vicious trade. He shows us nothing to forewarn us of the monumental destruction of which he is so capable of inflicting upon us, and in which he takes such absolute delight.

No, he is far too clever to expose himself, to let us see him for what he truly is until it is too late, until he has consumed us all and engulfed us in his wickedness and destroyed our once peaceful lives.

He takes our children's and the parents' present and future. He destroys our communities. He robs us of our money and jobs. He steals our self-esteem and dignity. He keeps us on a rollercoaster of emotions, of hope and fear.

Don't think for a second that he can't or won't invade your home. Don't think that you've locked all the doors and fastened all the windows and done everything you're supposed to do to prevent his unwelcome entrance into your lives. Oh no, he's already there, waiting to pounce. He stalks unrelentingly. He strikes when we're not looking, when we've let our guard down.

He is the Addiction Monster! And he comes in many forms. He befriends our children slowly and carefully, enticing them with empty promises of exciting highs. He depends on children's sense of invincibility and belief in their own immortality that they can trifle with him and remain untouched by his poison.

The Addiction Monster is an equal opportunity destroyer of lives, and not just the addicted people's lives. But the lives of everyone with whom he is intertwined, be it parents, spouse, children, siblings, friends, relatives or co-workers. Nobody is immune.

Nobody can escape the tentacles of the Addiction Monster. Like an octopus it wraps its deadly arms around us and consumes us all, either wittingly or unwittingly. Children from the right side of the tracks can be derailed by drugs. It happens all the time. The stereotypical image of the dysfunctional drug addict cloaked in the darkness of despair on the streets, quickly gives way to the boy and girl next door, the athlete, the musician, the smart kids, the good kids. These are your kids. These are my kids. These are everybody's kids. And they're dying in unprecedented numbers leaving sorrow and mass destruction in its wake.

Parents are not supposed to survive their children. It is not the natural order of things, but life takes strange and twisting turns along its path like a maze that we enter and have no idea where the end is or how to get there unscathed.

Many children succumb to the charms of the Addiction Monster because there is something lacking within them. Some have very low levels of dopamine, the "feel good" property of our brain. Some shake hands with the Addiction Monster because they think it's cool or because their friends entice them into doing so. Many children do so because they're trying to self-medicate their inner pain. Mental illness and drug addiction quite often go hand in hand.

But nobody welcomes the Addiction Monster into their life knowing how cruel and deadly this master is. Nobody thinks they will become addicted. Nobody wakes up one day and decides to be an addict. Who in their right mind would do that? The Addiction Monster just smiles and adds another name to his list of victims, nay, for each addicted person, he also adds the names of those other unwilling victims.

Nancy Reagan almost had it right with her "Just Say No" campaign during her husband, Ronald Reagan's presidency. A better mantra would have been "Just Say Know." Know what the Addiction Monster is really like. Know the havoc that he wreaks in everybody's lives. Know how he will enslave you, daring you to escape his death grip on you and laughing at each feeble attempt you make to free yourself from his choke hold.

The outlook for addicted people is very bleak. Nobody wants to hear that. It's too disheartening. But the recidivism rate for addicted people is an astounding 80 to 98%!! The Addiction Monster just revels in these statistics.

So what can you do to destroy this monster - this monster who is more vicious and cruel than any of the Chuckys or Freddys or Michael Myers' or Hannibal Lecters? How can you make sure he never seizes you in his grip and holds your head under water until your eyes start to bulge and you can't hold your breath any longer and then he releases you momentarily, only to plunge you into absolute fear and hopelessness again?

There is only one way, one sure, proven way to escape this horror and that is, of course, to never take that first step down that slippery slope! The Addiction Monster doesn't want you to know this. He wants you to think he's your friend, someone who will make you feel good and take you away from whatever miseries you think you have.

But you won't know true misery, true hell, or true hopelessness, until you have become a slave to the Addiction Monster. Once you've joined his legions, your life as you knew it will have evaporated into a dark, swirling mass of regrets and despair.

The choice is ours! Our future is in our hands. Don't let our present and our future be held captive by the Addiction Monster, for once he gains control over us, our chances of slaying him are bleak. Think about it.

Be smart - Don't start!

---

*"The sorrow which has no vent in tears
may make other organs weep."*

Henry Maudsley

OBERVATIONS OF A BEREAVED MOM

We Are One Voice

Upon re-reading I Am Your Disease (The Many Faces of Addiction)
I found out that we parents who lost their kids are of ONE voice.
The pictures and dates are different and the states and the names, but
that's all.
In a nutshell, this sums it up:
 All the parents feel they had to justify the idyllic upbringings of their
children.
Each carries guilt thinking every life setback for their kids triggered
use.
All naively believing their kids and that rehab was a cure-all.
Registered shock and horror that their kids died.
Disappointment with the system.
Acknowledging shame and stigma of others.
Missing their children and wanting them back for a second chance.
 It could have been written by one person and I share **all** those feel-
ings.
 It's amazing: we all have ONE voice with the same story repeat-
edly—the secrecy of usage by their kids—and death when they least
expected it.

*Linda – Mother of *Jake
*names changed to protect their privacy

"Just because you got the monkey off your back doesn't mean the circus has left town."

George Carlin, comedian

SCOTT'S STORY

Losing a child is one of the worst experiences that any human being can have. We all know that our life has to come to an end eventually and we mourn the passing of our parents and elderly aunts and uncles. As heartbreaking as this is, that is the life cycle. That is how it is supposed to be. We are not supposed to survive our child.

To lose a child is beyond cruel. It goes against all of our expectations of what life is supposed to be, how our lives are supposed to play out. It shatters our vision of the fairy tale existence that has been spoon-fed us since early childhood.

So when a beloved child dies, the fairy tale turns into a macabre nightmare, only this nightmare pervades our minds around the clock. There is no release from the tortured visions. Sleep only brings us more torment, where our mind plays horrific games and we have no control over what floats in and out of our heads.

Finally we awake with sudden relief that the nightmare is over, only to realize instantaneously that the nightmare was nothing more than a really bad dream and that the real nightmare, the real torture, the realization that this is really real, will rear its ugly head and keep us company all day and back into the night. We can't yearn for sweet sleep to escape our heartache because there is no surcease from this sorrow. Nighttime brings nightmares and daytime brings something much worse. It brings reality; a reality so horrible as to be almost incomprehensible.

My husband and I went through a living nightmare for 14 years as we helplessly watched our beloved youngest son fight, and eventually die from, an oftentimes fatal disease, quite often marked by vomiting, shaking, hallucinations, sunken in cheeks, and marathon sleeping sessions, alternating with days of sleeplessness. He contracted the disease when he was 17, when he had the world by the tail and so much life in front of him waiting to be enjoyed and grabbed with youthful gusto.

Our son had his own band. He played guitar. Actually he could play any musical instrument thrust into his hands, from the flute, to the drums, even a dulcimer, to the guitar. He had natural talent.

Scott lived life in the fast lane, enjoying all that life had to offer from bungee jumping, sky diving, to surfing in Australia and anything else that would afford him the adrenaline rush that he so craved. Is it any wonder he became a paramedic?

He also was one of the kindest, most compassionate people we've ever known. Animals were not possessions to him; they were creatures who needed love and care and kindness. Once you adopted one, you kept it. You did not "get rid of it" as many people do.

Our son had the all-American good looks, the buff physique honed from many years of surfing and working out with weights and running. His smile would knock your socks off. He was a Leo, exhibiting most of the traits of that Zodiac sign including the charm and charisma that left the girls spellbound. He had a brilliant mind with an IQ of 150 and even wrote professionally for a brief time.

During our son's illness, with its many remissions, he managed to become an EMT, graduating first in his class, and then on to become a Paramedic and then an RN. His ultimate goal was to be a physician. He would have made an excellent one too, not only for his sharp mind but also because of his kindness and compassion.

There were so many times during the years that our son could not attend various family functions due to his illness. He couldn't get out of bed. He didn't even graduate from high school, having missed so many days and because of the problems that his illness caused.

From the time he was 17 until he passed away on the night of December 1, 2002, at the age of 31, we didn't get much sleep. We were always waiting for the phone call that would tell us that our son had been taken to the hospital. We knew the disease was exacerbating and there was nothing that we could do. Still, you never really think it will happen. You are never prepared!

We had him in and out of institutions that specialized in his particular disease. We did everything humanly possible to save him. He also tried desperately to cure himself but all along he knew that it was a futile battle.

We spent untold thousands and thousands of dollars on treatments because no insurance company would pay for treatment for his type of disease. Had he been a leper he would have been treated better.

There was a time, not too terribly long ago, when cancer was spoken of in hushed tones. People who got cancer were sometimes ashamed, as were their relatives. Society placed a stigma on cancer victims and their families. I am old enough to remember this.

Then along came AIDS; another disease spoken of, in even more hushed tones than cancer.

People who smoked all their lives and contracted cancer were at first remonstrated for their vice which caused their condition. And we all know how AIDS victims were reviled in the '80s when first we heard of this devastating disease. Eventually, however, a collective common sense took over and we realized that these people were victims and deserved compassion and understanding.

I look forward to the day when the people who suffer from the disease that killed our son, will be accorded the same understanding and compassion as those other victims. As I stated earlier, our son developed his disease at the tender age of 17, when he was on the very brink of manhood, yet still a child, exploring, experimenting, and trying to find his way.

The institutions, of which I write, are in reality, rehab facilities. Our son died of the disease of addiction! Yes, addiction is a proven brain disease. The drugs change your brain's chemistry. What starts out as a lark, or a dare, or a curiosity or a way to self-medicate some inner turmoil, emotional pain or some form of mental illness, giving the person a deceptive sense of euphoria, soon gives way to despair, and if they're the unluckiest of the unlucky, to full-blown addiction.

For the majority of the addicted people there is no turning back. The Addiction Monster now has them in its clutches and it is a formidable foe, stronger than any parental admonitions, or books or TV shows or TV public service announcements, and much stronger than the hapless victim.

Most of us, well, let's face it, all of us make mistakes. Every single one of us makes many mistakes during our lifetime. Fortunately for us, most of our mistakes will be short-lived, cause no long-term consequences, and we can learn and profit from them and go on about our lives.

Our son was not perfect, not by any means. We do not look back at him through rose-colored glasses. We have chosen, however, to focus on the goodness that was him, his strengths and generosity and loving ways, and not to dwell on what the Addiction Monster did to him. We want him to be remembered for the kind person he was, not what the disease did to him.

Addiction usually does not afford us a second chance. It completely takes over the victim's mind and body. When you look into the face of your addicted child, you're not really seeing him or her. You are merely seeing a shell that resembles your child, because hidden inside is the Monster who is calling all the shots. As much as your child tries to fight this monster, most of the time he doesn't have a chance. The Monster is strong, tenacious, unrelenting, and lulls the child into the false hope that just one more hit will make him feel better and then he can start fighting the Monster again. But it doesn't always work this way. The Monster will win almost every time. Its strength is Herculean.

It's easy to cast aspersions on the addicted person, to look down our noses at them, and to say that they made their bed, let them lie in it. Would we say this about the cancer victims? Although AIDS patients still experience a certain amount of hostility and lack of understanding by the general public, their plight is gradually becoming more understood. Progress is finally being made in this regard.

Now it's time, actually way past time, for all of us to understand addiction. Addiction is not a conscious choice. The experimentation which usually begins in childhood indeed is a conscious choice, but addiction is not.

Children take drugs before their brains are fully developed. We don't have the tools to make smart decisions...but we think we do. And that is our downfall. Children make mistakes. That's a part of growing up.

The lucky ones will be able to overcome these childhood mistakes and grow up and go on to lead happy, productive lives.

As my son used to tell me, "Mom, nobody wakes up one day and decides to be an addict." I'd like to add that nobody wakes up one day and decides to be a bereaved parent, yet it is thrust upon us with all the weight of the world. We are victims too of our drug-entrenched society. Addiction is a family disease!

As much as we bereaved parents suffer, and believe me we suffer inconsolably, our children suffered 10 fold. They never expected it to happen to them. They didn't know what they were up against. They didn't realize the searing pain they would cause us, the pain that would live with us every second of every day.

We miss our son more than mere words can ever express, as any parent who has survived their child can attest to. Every sunrise that breaks, every sunset, every spring when all the flowers bloom and trees break into leaf, every Christmas, his birthday, every discovery of a former friend of his who has married or has had a child, every life event that others take for granted, all of these weigh heavily upon our hearts knowing that these experiences are lost to him forever; and to us.

We are not angry with our son for his choices. Many parents hold on to a strong anger about what their child did and how their behavior robbed the family of its future. We wouldn't be angry with our child if he had developed cancer because he smoked cigarettes or he became a paraplegic because of excessive risk-taking behavior. So we feel no anger, just incredible sadness for him, for all he lost.

Our only consolation is that he is no longer suffering. His pain has ended. Ours endures.

> *"We each are faced with choices every day. Every day is a new beginning. We cannot alter our past, nor can we assure our future. All we have is today. But how we act today can impact our future positively or negatively."*
>
> **Sheryl Letzgus McGinnis**

*"There is no pain so great as the memory
of joy in present grief."*

Aeschylus, Greek Playwright

ADVICE FROM PARENTS TO OTHER PARENTS

ADVICE FROM PARENTS TO OUR YOUTH

ADVICE AND SUGGESTIONS

The following chapter contains truly heartfelt advice by those of us who have been there, done that. We're not trying to tell you how to raise your child. What we are doing is offering our experiences to you, our newfound knowledge (sadly, a lot of it learned after the death of our child), our discoveries and whatever wisdom we have gained while walking this torturous path.

If any of our thoughts and words help you, then in turn we are helped. We cannot reclaim our lost child but perhaps we can help spare you from living our nightmare. This is our goal and for many of us it is our passion. It is the chance to reach out to others, to give our children a legacy, to let their words speak to you, and to afford them some dignity.

COCAINE

Cocaine is a powerfully addictive stimulant drug. The powdered, hydrochloride salt form of cocaine can be snorted or dissolved in water and injected. Crack is cocaine that has not been neutralized by an acid to make the hydrochloride salt. This form of cocaine comes in a rock crystal that can be heated and its vapors smoked. The term "crack" refers to the crackling sound heard when it is heated.

Regardless of how cocaine is used or how frequently, a user can experience acute cardiovascular or cerebrovascular emergencies, such as a heart attack or stroke, which could result in sudden death. Cocaine-related deaths are often a result of cardiac arrest or seizure followed by respiratory arrest.

—NIDA   (NATIONAL INSTITUTE ON DRUG ABUSE)

THOUGHTS FROM KAREN — MOTHER OF GINO

Although it's been almost 6 years since I lost my son Gino to a heroin overdose I can remember the chaos and isolation and insanity as clear as if it was yesterday.

I think the number one thing I would tell a parent living with an addicted person would be to seek help and support from outside sources for themselves.

Addiction, although it's been proven to be a brain disease, is the only disease that isn't looked at as a disease but rather a life style choice.

The only person a parent or loved one can help in this disease is themselves and it's so frustrating.

I know for myself I enabled my son. I used to hate the word enable because I didn't truly understand what enabling was.

A perfect example of enabling for me would be when Gino would get into trouble. He would get arrested and the first one he would call would be his father and me. He would plead for us to bail him out of jail, going on and on about how if he doesn't get out of jail he's going to lose his job and he won't be able to find another one. He would play on my sympathy. No sooner did we bail him out than he was out using drugs again.

As a mother I wanted to spare him the pain and assumed if I helped him he would have a better chance with recovery if the hole he was digging wasn't too deep. I now know that the addict has to suffer the consequences of their actions because if they don't there wouldn't be a reason for them to stop abusing drugs.

Also parents need to understand that addiction doesn't discriminate. It touches the young, rich, poor, white, black, yellow, big, small; No one is immune to it affecting their family.

There is one more thing I would like to tell mothers and fathers about trusting their intuition. When our children were growing up we trusted our intuition to help us do what was best for them. When they get older I know I had intuitions of what was going on with my son but I think I didn't want to accept how serious his drug addiction was.

He was so good at convincing me I was the crazy one, that he wasn't using drugs and I was just way out in left field with my thoughts.

"Most of the important things in the world have been accomplished by people who have kept on trying when there seemed to be no hope at all."

Dale Carnegie, motivational author and speaker

Thoughts from Paul
— Father of Josh

Josh always said, "Do you think I want to be an addict? I have no choice. I no longer get high. This just makes me feel normal."

I always had a feeling he was dealing on the side. Last week I sat with a girl and her mother who knew Josh. She told me she asked Josh to get her drugs. He refused and told her not to get involved so I am proud that he would not sell to just anyone. She also told me she reads his poem every morning and evening and it is what has kept her clean for the last 9 months.

I think Josh was ashamed of himself, but on the same token I believe he was self medicating for an issue that I never knew about.

When we went to family counseling, when Josh was in the first re-hab, the doctor told me I put the wrong child in therapy. The fact that when I got divorced Josh really didn't respond showed he needed the therapy, not my daughter who threatened suicide at the time. He could never tell me why after being clean for months at a time he kept going back; the pull of the drugs was just so strong. Of course, as a person who never used, I could never understand. But the key is, no one starts with the thought of becoming an addict. And once it starts, it's like a train going downhill; there is very little chance of stopping.

My first thing I would say to parents is to get a safe or a lockbox. All medications such as Vicodin, and Percocet, etc, anything that can be abused needs to be placed in the safe.

If the grades slip, the friends change, go with your suspicions, because they are probably right. Immediately, if you feel something has changed go to the drug store, they sell urine drug tests over the counter and test your child. If they are not using they won't care, and if they are you will know right away, before it is too late.

I accepted every story Josh told me in the beginning; the drugs weren't his, he was holding them for someone, etc. When he was arrested I posted bail and hired an attorney. I should have never done that. A little jail might have helped; tough love is something I should have practiced.

I hate to say this, but if you think they are using you must search their rooms, pull out the drawers and look underneath them, look in the closet, the attic, etc. After he passed I found the hiding spots. Steroids are drugs. They are not harmless. We have members of Families Changing America who have lost their children to steroids.

"No one feels another's grief, no one understands another's joy. People imagine they can reach one another. In reality they only pass each other by."

Franz Schubert

Thoughts from Sandi
– Mother of Robby

I would tell parents to trust their gut feelings no matter what your kid or anyone else tells you. If you think your kid is using some drug, most likely he is. Earlier and longer treatment is better and do NOT trust them for years, no matter how well they seem to be doing. They can't even trust themselves, though they won't tell you that. Stick to your child and their treatment plan. If they say they don't need it anymore, don't believe it. Use your parental control for as long as you are able. You are not supposed to be your child's best friend. This is not about YOU, it is about your child's disease and the stakes are high! And, always remember that Tough Love means you still love them unconditionally and you let them know it, no matter what.

After a relapse, I found my son sobbing. He was saying, "Mom, I just want my life back! I want to be a kid again! I am so sorry, I don't know if I can ever do this!" I had never, ever seen my teenage son cry this hard, not since he was an infant.

Kids need self confidence and they need to know the real truth about all drugs so they feel strong enough to really say no to drugs. They need to hear this type of truthful information from the time they are very young. A kid who feels they can tell a parent anything may feel stronger telling kids he isn't interested in drugs because he can share what happens with a trusted parent.

Robby was a happy and healthy little boy, the baby of the family. Everyone who knew him always said he was sweet. He was very empathetic and cared about people and animals. His emotional difficulties came from a father who favored his older brother. The more Robby failed at trying to please his dad, the better he felt at pleasing his friends. They were everything to him. When the guys all started using drugs, he told me he didn't want them to think he was a wimp, so he meant to use a few times and quit. He had no idea that he would not be able to quit. He hated himself for who he was becoming while trying to support his heroin habit. I don't know if he ever got his self esteem back.

"Drugs are a bet with your mind."

Jim Morrison, singer, poet, songwriter

Thoughts from Linda*
— Mother of Jake*

(*names changed to protect their privacy)

The things persons with this brain disease of addiction say are all similar. It's no longer about sane thinking, prudence, etc. once the brain has been under siege. It becomes one-tracked.

I am understanding more and more about the disease. It is truly a disease that has nothing to do with family/environment (although addicted persons often talk of triggers…if it isn't one thing it would be another anyway).

The disease of addiction is a stand alone illness that comes from something within, a distorted self image, super extraordinary sensitivity to life's disappointments (super is key word), and need to do something about it, taking matters into their own hands.

It's a very human thing to want escape and relief, it's just that in many instances, it turns into a full blown illness. That parts of their brains that don't feel good to begin with, get hooked, like magnets to things that make them feel great for a while, then rob them. It is truly a psychic cancer. It's truly a mysterious one, like physical cancer, put into the person from without, whereas cancer develops within, though we aren't sure of that one either, and in some cases, not!

I now prefer the term, persons with addictions, or addicted persons, or persons with brain diseases. I think it helps remove the stigma. Just like society stopped calling disabled people 'handicapped'--they are now persons with disabilities...I like this all much better. And mentally retarded. (another stigma term) became developmentally disabled.

When your beloved child, your own flesh and blood, wants to change his or her consciousness, and be somewhere else and begins to love that altered realm over life itself, and refuses to return to where you are, it creates panic in a parent. Instead of ministering to the sick, as you would with other illnesses, you sometimes wind up fighting with your own child. Sometimes your child takes off and disappears for days or more...jail, a hospital, an obscure street, a morgue.

When your child takes poison repeatedly to cope with living or because some part of his brain malfunctions or because he just likes getting high, or because he feels hopelessly hooked, you rip your guts out and stuff them back inside yourself, trying to save them from themselves. Sooner or later that child self destructs right in front of you while your hands are tied. It's one of the cruelest experiences any parent can ever suffer.

Although addiction is recognized as a disease like any other, the child has still had some hand in creating and maintaining that addiction disease and in his own demise. That is what is so profoundly injurious. It is the antithesis of what a parent thinks a parent should be .When bearing witness to a child in the throes of addiction and not being able to do a damned thing about it, your hands are tied....it's as if a sword were dangling from the ceiling over your head.

It's hard sometimes to see addiction-overdose-intoxication as a natural cause of death, one that seems like it should have been so preventable. How silly. How hideous. You mull over how and when addiction somehow stepped in between the family vacations and togetherness, in between the bedtime stories and the hugs, in between Little League or Ballet lessons and the drug prevention programs in school. Is this from genes, how could this be, you angst.

Medical science gives us hope that there will be answers and treatments one day and some of us cling to faith in a Higher Power, or God, as well. I think it also helps that we refer to the afflicted as 'persons with addiction' rather than 'addicts'. Addicts don't get any respect. It really upsets me when I hear the words "He was a good kid. He didn't do drugs." This implies that kids who do drugs are NOT good kids! Well they ARE good kids, as good as any other. You just have to look a little deeper sometimes, under the debris of the illness. They're our kids, yours and mine. I hate the words, drug addict, because they strike terror in my heart. If I say brain diseased or addicted, I feel MUCH better. The stigma lies in me, too.

ADVICE FROM CELESTE — MOTHER OF BRANDON

It seems the signs are the same with all the addicted children. They become very good at lying and denial of any faults. They have extreme highs and lows that change in a matter of minutes. Look for excessive talking, scratching and forgetfulness. Sudden rashes may appear and they usually refuse any treatment. Their ability to reason and tolerate any change in family routine is gone. Confusion becomes a daily thing and paranoia is always with them.

They have been wronged and we become the bad guys simply because we are there and there has to be a "Bad Guy." They often transfer their addiction to us. We are the addicts in their minds. One drink and we become "Alcoholics." They become the VICTIM, simply because there has to be one. I don't know how to advise other parents still going through this. Nothing I did worked. Just love them, hold them, and fight for them with all you have. If you lose this fight, you need to know you did all you could.

> *"My grief lies all within, and these external manners of lament are merely shadows to the unseen grief that swells with silence in the tortured soul."*
>
> **William Shakespeare**

OxyContin

"Stopping the spread of OxyContin abuse has been difficult because in the five or so years it has been available it has become very popular with doctors and patients. It does its job well. Because so many prescriptions have been written for real medical complaints, the potential supply of the drug to drug abusers is very high.

What YOU need to know about experimenting with OxyContin is that it's just like playing with heroin, cocaine, methamphetamine, or a loaded gun: Deadly."

InTheKnowZone.com

Street Names for Oxycontin:

Kicker, OC, Oxy, OX, Blue, Oxycotton, Hillybilly Heroin

usdoj.gov/dea

Thoughts from Ginger – Mother of Gene

I believe that my son, Gene, was taken from this world because his tender heart could not bear the injustices of it. I believe that seeing people suffer and struggle to survive was too much for him, and a large part of what caused him to turn to heroin.

He had three simple goals in his life, often repeated to me over the years. And when he was taken from me at the age of 23, he had accomplished them all. To be married, to have a child, and to have a dog of his own; that was all he wanted out of life.

Before any of these three things had happened in his life, but after he had come under the grip of drug and alcohol addiction, he was in a car accident. We met him at the hospital in the wee hours of New Year's Eve day, where he received forty stitches in his face. No other injuries. Then we went to see the site of the crash.

The earth of a high bank on a curve was gouged and scraped and cut, and a road sign was demolished. Then we went to see the car. There was nothing on that car that was salvageable, inside or out.

He had hit ice going way too fast on a nasty curve, and the car had flipped end-over-end and rolled side-over-side, and had come to rest on the roof. The only thing that saved him was the fact that he always kept his seat headrest up as far as it would go, even though he was 5' 8" tall and didn't really need it up that far. The headrest held, and kept the roof from crushing him. It was amazing. That headrest should have never held the car up.

He should have never walked away from that wreck. But walk away he did, because on that lonely back road, he had to walk to the nearest farmhouse for help.

Why was he able to walk away? Because he had a tender heart which

49

only asked three things from life - a wife, a child, and a dog - and he did not have them yet, and he was worthy of having them. The wife came first, then the dog, and lastly, the little girl. She was just nine months old when he died.

Even in something that has shredded my own heart, is the evidence of God's goodness, and that He will give us our heart's desire. God knew that Gene could take no more of the suffering and struggling of this world, including his own addictions, and after fulfilling those three simple requests, He took him home, where he would suffer and struggle no more.

"Persons aged 26 or older who initiated use of prescription psychotherapeutic drugs before age 16 were more likely than persons who initiated use at later ages to continue to be users in the past year" (2004).

SAMHSA (Department of Health and Human Services)

Thoughts from Angie — Mother of Michael

I believe kids do the drugs to eliminate the ways they feel like failures… whether it's with school, friends, girls/boys, social scenes… life issues, divorce of parents, trouble with DUI's whatever the case.

I believe they start as a way to get rid of the pain / hurts on a temporary basis and pretty soon it becomes the only way they know how to exist on a day to day basis.

Parents — educate yourself —About drugs, alcohol, FRIENDS… if your gut tells you something is not right, it's probably not… go with your instinct. Don't live in denial… it's the worse possible thing. Go to whatever length you have to help your child. Don't believe their lies… they are masters at the lies. I lived in such denial that my son had more than a problem with alcohol and marijuana.

I was nosey. I searched, I questioned, I did everything I thought was within my power. A lot of it was Michael covering, he knew I was looking. All the friends covered and never said a word about anything. They lied for him as well. I would have sought outside help more than I did. I would have been more stern about my rules.

But Michael always made a believer out of me. He had a way about him when it came to the lies. I wish I realized the depression he was in several times that was so severe was all related to the drugs. I thought it was simple depression. When we put him in lockdown for suicidal thoughts and the doctor dismissed him after 24 hours saying he has a substance abuse problem and that's the problem and he doesn't want help, I thought he was a complete idiot. I took Michael to another doctor to treat for the depression but I did not follow through with the substance abuse issue because Michael told me he wanted no help. Again, I thought it was only drinking and pot. That's what he made me believe and I'd never seen anything different.

Drug using friends, generally will hang you out to dry if it means they might get into trouble.

> *"What this power is I cannot say; all I know is that it exists and it becomes available only when a man is in that state of mind in which he knows exactly what he wants and is fully determined not to quit until he finds it."*
>
> **Alexander Graham Bell**

Thoughts From Shirley
— Mother of Travis

The one thing I can give advice on is to KNOW ALL THE SYMP-
TOMS OF DRUG USE! IF YOU SUSPECT ANYTHING, please
confront your child. They may be desperately seeking help on the inside, but afraid to talk about it to their parents, as they may be
ashamed and have no hope.

> *"The idea that addiction is somehow a psychological illness is, I think, totally ridiculous. It's as psychological as malaria. It's a matter of exposure. People, generally speaking, will take any intoxicant or any drug that gives them a pleasant effect if it is available to them."*
>
> **William S. Burroughs - author**

METHAMPHETAMINE

Methamphetamine is a very addictive stimulant drug that activates certain systems in the brain. It is chemically related to amphetamine but, at comparable doses, the effects of methamphetamine are much more potent, longer lasting, and more harmful to the central nervous system (CNS).

Methamphetamine is a Schedule II stimulant, which means it has a high potential for abuse and is available only through a prescription that cannot be refilled. It can be made in small, illegal laboratories, where its production endangers the people in the labs, neighbors, and the environment. Street methamphetamine is referred to by many names, such as "speed," "meth," and "chalk." Methamphetamine hydrochloride, clear chunky crystals resembling ice, which can be inhaled by smoking, is referred to as "ice," "crystal," "glass," and "tina."

NIDA (NATIONAL INSTITUTE ON DRUG ABUSE

Thoughts from DuVette — Mother of Anna

Know you can say No!

Because I did not know my child was going through such turmoil with her soul, I thought everything was fine.

I grew up with the "Cleaver Syndrome." That is to say, I thought my children would be like Wally and Theodore. Needless to say they were not.

I regret never listening to my children when they would come to me with petty grievances and complaints. They were crying out for help and I didn't know it. My regret seems to add up to my loss, and I can never forgive myself.

It was up to me to give my children the power to overcome the lack of self-esteem that drove them to drug use. I can never forgive myself.

"Drugs are a waste of time. They destroy your memory and your self-respect and everything that goes along with your self-esteem."

Kurt Cobain, singer, musician

ALCOHOL

"Because the liver is the chief organ responsible for metabolizing alcohol, it is especially vulnerable to alcohol-related injury. Liver cirrhosis is a major cause of death in the United States."

US Department of Health and Human Services

"Children who begin drinking alcohol before the age of 15 are 5 times more likely than those who start after age 21 to develop alcohol problems."

www.samhsa.gov

Thoughts from Sandy — Mother of Jason

I can remember several times in my son Jason's life when I caught him getting high. The first time he was in junior high. I found out he was smoking pot and I had a talk with him about it. I explained that it would interfere with his motivation and lead him to other things he didn't need to have in his life. I wasn't just talking about drugs but other bad decisions. I told him that once you made that choice to say yes to one thing you knew you shouldn't be doing, it made it easier to say yes to more and more things. Saying no was always the best way of assuring that you made the right choice.

Did that help – no, I don't think it did. I didn't really know what to say to my son. I now think that the issue of smoking pot or using a drug is deeper than the drug itself. What I didn't ask my son was why he was using it. I didn't ask him if there was something in his life that he was trying to mask. I didn't ask because I didn't know then about self-medicating. I didn't know as much about drugs as I thought I knew, and I was myself a child of the 60's and 70's after all.

When Jason became a young adult I knew he and the gang of kids that always hung out around the house were smoking pot. Sometimes taking LSD and eating mushrooms. I am not proud to say that or that we had done it when we were kids too. He got the lectures about not wanting illegal drugs in my house, and the lectures about risking jail. I guess that somehow in all the years I had been exposed to drugs I had never known anyone who died from them or anyone at that time who was an addict. That was then…

When I realized that Jason's life had been taken over by drugs was when his life long best friend was murdered at the age of 19. It was devastating for Jason. Jason asked to talk to me and we went into my room. Jason told me that he and Joey had been selling LSD. Joey was murdered by someone they knew because the kid didn't get high on the LSD they had sold him. That was when I first knew that drugs had taken over my son's life and this was bigger than getting high once in a while watching Saturday Night Live. Everything changed from that point on.

I had several talks with my son about why he used after Joey's death. Jason told me that the only time he felt normal was when he was high. Jason suffered from depression and had always been a shy, withdrawn kid. He explained that he self-medicated to forget, to feel normal, to be able to feel happy and relaxed. He believed that getting high led him to a more spiritual level and that he thought pot and LSD made you a better, more spiritual person. Jason thought if the world smoked pot and tripped a few times there would be no more war, or violence.

It was a warped way of thinking because the drugs had warped the way he thought, the way his brain processed thoughts, and created false beliefs. It was that tune in and tune out attitude of my generation but today's drugs were much more potent and destructive than the drugs the hippies in my time were experimenting with. Things got to a point where it was just a waste of time to try and reason with him. I remember thinking "Wow, he is just really out there." So I just looked after him and prayed for the best. I hoped that if I could keep him alive till he turned 30 then he would grow up and grow out of this as did my generation.

After Joey's murder Jason spiraled deeper and deeper into drugs of all kinds. Eventually he became addicted to cocaine and went into rehab for five months. He had admitted to himself that drugs had taken over his life. In the 16 months that followed rehab Jason had gotten his life back on track, back in college, and back on the road to a good life for the first time. We both began to believe he was going to make it. But that was not meant to be.

On February 28th, 1998, five years after the murder of his best friend, my son lost his life. For reasons I will never know any real answers to my son decided to take LSD one afternoon. While left alone on a bad LSD trip, my son climbed out of a third story window trying to escape his hallucinations. Jason fell and shattered his skull on the concrete sidewalk at the entrance of the building. Jason was pronounced brain dead hours later at the trauma center. The next day Jason was removed from life support and passed away.

It has been 10 years since my son lost his life, 15 years since his best friend Joey was murdered. Out of five boys that pretty much lived in my house, that worried me sick, that ran me crazy, only one is still alive today. I am happy to say that he has turned his life around. I am proud of him.

I am tired of burying children. I am tired of crying everyday for the loss of my son's life. The devastation his drug addiction took on our lives didn't end when he died. It won't end until I die or until the last of his friends who loved him and were so heartbroken when he died are all long gone too. It won't end until everyone who loved him, and miss him terribly all these years are finally gone ourselves.

I have tried to tell the truth here because it is so important not to cover up our mistakes. Not to lie about something that takes the lives of our children - one every twenty minutes. I make no excuses for my son or myself. We just did the best we could with the knowledge we had at the time. I hope that knowledge will save lives in the future. Knowledge about the disease of addiction is the only hope humanity may have.

A thought on "telling on friends." They don't want to expose their friends' deep secret and ruin their reputation. This has to be done in prevention, the training them that saving a life is more important than saving a reputation. Many parents themselves don't admit to others their children have drug problems. You don't have to die before you live!

"No greater grief than to remember days of gladness when sorrow is at hand."

Friedrich von Schiller

INHALANTS

"One of the most dangerous substances abused by children and teens may be found in the home. These toxic substances are collectively referred to as inhalants - breathable chemical vapors that produce mind-altering effects. A variety of common products contain substances that can be inhaled. Many people do not think that products such as spray paints, nail polish remover, hair spray, glues, and cleaning fluids present any risk of abuse, because their intoxicating effects are so totally unconnected to their intended uses. Yet, young children and adolescents are among those most likely to abuse them, and do seek them out for this purpose. Adults should store household products carefully to prevent accidental inhalation; they should also remain aware of the temptations that these dangerous substances pose to children in their homes."

"Most inhalant abusers are younger than age 25. One national survey indicates that about 3 percent of U.S. children have tried inhalants by the time they reach fourth grade.
Eighth-graders generally abuse at higher rates than 10th- or 12th-graders.
In 2004, 8th-grade girls reported more inhalant abuse than boys, while 12th-grade boys reported more than girls"

NIDA (NATIONAL INSTITUTE ON DRUG ABUSE)

Thoughts from Pam
— Mother of Maria

Always remember, our kids used RECREATIONALLY, and they thought they could handle it; the fact that they were bright, or had so much to lose, or had the attention from the opposite sex, and the support and chances they did, just goes to show you that the ones who "have it all going for them" want to explore everything!

They get intrigued, and all the media hype in the last 20 years via the music, the stars, the films, the millionaire rappers out of jail, the glamorous girlfriends of the macho drug dealers in films, all the songs written about how cool it is to be stoned, my God, it was like soaking up the culture for them, and it's getting worse! You can't watch stand-up comedic material without listening to a "supposedly hilarious" drug story!

I can't tell you how many drop dead gorgeous males AND females I have known through the years, who got high before going out socially to boost their confidence! The more attention they got, naturally the more they questioned it, and didn't want to take "any chances" that the admiration might slip away!

The younger the age for the onset of drug abuse proves again and again that the user never "grows up" emotionally; they stay the age they were when they started. I have seen it again and again, hence, our kids thinking they were invulnerable, and weren't going to run out of chances!

When you're a teen you think you have a whole lifetime to straighten your life out, and the last thing you think about is how any mistake will haunt you for the rest of your life, to say nothing of using drugs!

NICOTINE

One of the most heavily used addictive drugs in the U.S.

Nicotine is highly addictive. The tar in cigarettes increases a smoker's risk of lung cancer, emphysema, and bronchial disorders. The carbon monoxide in smoke increases the chance of cardiovascular diseases. Secondhand smoke causes lung cancer in adults and greatly increases the risk of respiratory illnesses in children.

Thoughts from Alice
— Mother of Danny

Suspicious things found in their bedrooms.

I had found once in awhile cigarette lighters that were always broken and or disassembled (purpose - make flame higher, they tweak the lighter used for crack and or melting heroin) tin foil gum wrappers shaped like a funnel, and gutted pens (used for smoking coke, crack, heroin) and most of all count your spoons.

I've found very creative bongs and what not, soda cans, plastic bottle and toilet paper rolls. Also hiding spots, in clothes pockets, in shoes, inside light switch covers, drop ceilings, under wall to wall carpet, see if it has been tampered with. Under lamps, trophies, stuffed animals, etc., etc. they are creative with hiding spots too.

"Instead of weeping when a tragedy occurs in a songbird's life, it sings away its grief. I believe we could well follow the pattern of our feathered friends."

Unknown

---

*"Let's put a drug court in our community.
Let's make sure that everybody, rich or poor, no matter
where they're from, male or female, has an opportunity to
be healed no matter, rather than punished."*

**Martin Sheen, Actor
From Eonline.com June 22, 1998**

Thoughts from Pam — Mother of Keith

Giving advice to parents is so hard for me. I couldn't save Keith, how in the world am I going to try to help someone else's child? Well we have to try. We cannot give up on our children. If there was ONE way to save our children from addiction we wouldn't have this problem. What works in one situation may not work in another. You have to put on a full battle armor and do everything you can to help your child.

Education is the number one thing I would say. Too many Parents are in denial. Get online and look up every drug that is around. Know what the signs are and what different drugs look or smell like. It's okay if your child hates you when you raid their room. Check out who their friends are. Drop by that party that so and so's parents are supposed to be supervising.

Talk to your child EVERYDAY about peer pressure. Together think of ways for them to avoid these situations or be able to say no thanks, I don't need drugs in my life. It is so hard being a teen these days. Raising four sons I witnessed them all go through so much. Other kids can be so cruel and it's no fun being the one picked on or left out. Keith always felt like he didn't fit in and everyone was waiting for him to leave so the real party could start. This he told me after he started getting high. At first they feel everything is so much easier to deal with when they are high but that soon changes. Depression will eventually take over and many other mood changes.

This is the hardest thing a Parent will go through except of course the death of your child. Love your child no matter what but you do not have to love what they are doing. You have to be tough and let them know you will not stand by and watch them slowly kill himself. It is true: you really can Love Your Child To Death!! Get out of denial! It doesn't matter what anyone says or thinks, this can happen to any family so never blame yourself. What's important is helping your child live!

And again, there is not one answer. Try every thing you can but one thing you have to keep in mind. Addicts are the best liars out there. Don't believe half of what they tell you. This is the drugs talking. You also have to take care of yourself. Going thru this will drain every ounce of energy out of you.

The best advice I can give is educate yourself while your kids are still young. Teach them what drugs can and will do when they are young. Don't wait until this horrible disease knocks on your door and catches you off guard. Be ready and waiting because no one ever thinks this will happen to their child.

Teach your child at a very young age and keep telling them it's okay to tell your friends NO. We teach our children to not talk to strangers and tell them about the dangerous people in this world. Well now we have to teach them about a danger that one day chances are very high they will have to deal with. Drugs are in every school, every neighborhood and there is no place to hide from them. Teach them that it will most likely be someone they think is their friend. Let them know sometimes friends make big mistakes. Teach them to walk away from a situation they know is wrong. A real friend will understand.

Keith was my oldest of four sons. He grew up in a nice middle class neighborhood. Had both parents and I was a stay at home Mom. We were a very close family. We spent years on baseball fields, football fields, ate dinner together and did all the things they say will help keep your kids off drugs. Well it didn't keep our child off drugs. It started with alcohol at a party then went on and on. Two years later Keith died from a heroin overdose at the age of 18. Keith was not addicted to one drug; he would try whatever was around and one night it was a mixture of drugs. Again starting with alcohol.

If I could go back in time I would have taught him about drugs at a young age. I would have checked out what he was doing more than I did. I would follow through on many of the things I said, not just threaten. I was always the easy parent. It was always "Wait until your Dad gets home." Then half the time I wouldn't tell Dad.

Now our family is forever changed. We are very close still but there is always that empty chair and all of us wondering…What would Keith think?

> *"Suppressed grief suffocates, it rages within the breast, and is forced to multiply its strength."*
>
> **Ovid, Roman poet**

"Pharmaceutical companies will soon rule the world if we keep letting them believe we are a happy, functional society so long as all the women are on Prozac, all children on Ritalin, and all men on Viagra".

The Quote Garden

Thoughts from Lucille
— Mother of Lenny

Lenny always said that he never thought that he would get addicted to drugs because of his uncle being a heroin addict. He also said that he didn't like what drugs took from him:

> Family
> Friends
> Money
> Trust
> Possessions

He also said that he didn't do this to hurt me.

Listen to your kids!! Take medications to control your anxiety if you need to. See your doctor and discuss this with him/her.

> *"To spare oneself from grief at all cost can be achieved only at the price of total detachment, which excludes the ability to experience happiness."*
>
> **Erich Fromme**

"Grief and sadness knits two hearts in closer bonds than happiness ever can; and common sufferings are far stronger than common joys."

Alphonse de Lamartine

Thoughts from Sherry — Mother of Scott

My input in our family dynamics was to raise our two boys as I was raised back in the 50s and 60s – with trust. My parents trusted me and I rarely gave them any reasons to regret the trust they placed in me.

I wanted us to raise our two boys the same way, with trust and confidence.

I learned a big lesson (with my youngest son at least) – that times are different now. We can't have blind faith and trust in our children. We have to always maintain vigilance and be very aware of the dangers that face our children today.

We can still trust our children but with an always questioning mind as to what is really going on in their lives. We can't let our guard down. We can't be our children's friend. We are their parents! We are the ones our children turn to for guidance and for discipline.

Scott always considered me his "best friend." He freely and gladly told others this. I have to admit there were many times that I responded to his problems more as a friend than his parent. In retrospect, this was very wrong.

Children have friends of their own. They don't need their parents to be their friend. But one of the most important words of advice I can give, is to get to know your child's friends and if possible, get to know their parents.

When they become teens, the inevitable sleepovers will start. Quite often they're innocent fun. But many times the sleepovers are just excuses for each child to tell their parents that they're sleeping at so and so's house. In reality, they could be off running around all night, partying, driving, perhaps drinking and driving, drugging and driving or any number of unsavory activities.

If your child tells you they're spending the night with their friend, don't be embarrassed or afraid to call the house and speak to the parents. This is a time when your child will question your trust in them with the "Don't you trust me?" whine. We're torn because we want to trust them, they've never given us any reason not to trust them and we don't want to embarrass them in front of their friends by calling their parents. I think this might be especially hard for the boys because they don't want to be seen as "mama's boys." Do it anyway!! Call the parents!

If you have any inkling that your child might be doing drugs, this is the time to pull out all the stops. If, after all the good conversations you've had with them, the promises extracted from them, you still get that "hinky" feeling that something might be wrong, go with your gut instinct.

Listen in on their conversations with friends. Check their drawers, their closets, their book bags, etc. Yes, this sounds horrible on the surface and indeed it is! Nobody wants to be a cop to their child.

But we're talking about saving lives here! When I first discovered the "Chore Boy" scrubbers in my son's room, I believed whatever flimsy excuse he gave me for having them. (It wasn't until much later that I learned these are used as filters for smoking crack). No, I didn't do any research on this. How stupid was that? I would urge you not to repeat my stupidity.

So in essence, arm yourself with knowledge. Learn all about drug paraphernalia, what it looks like, what it's called. Educate yourself on all things drugs. Why shouldn't you? Your child is certainly learning all that he/she can about drugs. Only they're learning ways to get high. You can't let them get one step ahead of you.

Whatever the outcome is in your own situation, I would advise every parent to always let their child know they are loved! No matter what! Loving them won't stop them from doing drugs but if your child should ultimately die from drug abuse, you'll know that they carried your love for them to the grave.

Our son knew he was loved. We hated the drugs but we loved him and it's some consolation to us now that he carried our love with him.

Our son was an avid reader ever since he first learned how. He loved literature and some of his favorite authors were Ayn Rand, John Steinbeck, Mark Twain, Kurt Vonnegut, Henry David Thoreau, the three Bronte' sisters and in keeping with his whimsical side, the poet, Shel Silverstein whom I quote here. Scott would appreciate that.

"Listen to the mustn'ts, child. Listen to the don'ts. Listen to the shouldn'ts, the impossibles, the won'ts. Listen to the never haves, then listen close to me…Anything can happen, child. Anything can be."

Shel Silverstein, poet, cartoonist and composer.

MDMA (ECSTASY)

(XTC, X, ADAM, ROLL, HUG, BEANS, LOVE DRUG)

"Short term effects — Users report intensely pleasurable effects – including an enhanced sense of self-confidence, and energy. Effects include feelings of peacefulness, acceptance and empathy. Users say they experience feelings of closeness with others and a desire to touch others. Other effects can include involuntary teeth clenching, loss of inhibitions, transfixion on sights and sounds, nausea, blurred vision, chills, and/or sweating. Increases in heart rate and blood pressure, as well as seizures, are also possible. The stimulant effects of the drug enable users to dance for extended periods, which when combined with the hot crowded conditions usually found at raves, can lead to severe dehydration and hyperthermia or dramatic increases in body temperature. This can lead to muscle breakdown and kidney, liver and cardiovascular failure. Cardiovascular failure has been reported in some of the Ecstasy-related fatalities. After-effects can include sleep problems, anxiety and depression."

Drugfree.org

Partnership For A Drug-Free America

Thoughts from Jack — Father of Scott

The most difficult thing about being a parent of an addicted person is not knowing what to do about it. Having been there, my first impulse was to feel sorry for my child and get professional help. After exhausting my insurance and my son having a wonderful time on his vacation in rehab this did absolutely nothing.

Then came the hand wringing and the anxiety of what to do next. This of course did absolutely nothing either. The anger followed and the results were the same. After all of that I thought maybe I could be a better father and get my son more involved with me in some sort of personal way. I took him camping only to find out that the island we spent the night on had him sneaking to the other end of the island as I prepared supper while he did his drugs. I tried to get him involved in building a boat but he was never there to give me help and my mind had thoughts of chaining him to the floor. This of course might have worked but I knew it was not the answer.

I tried more love and help and found out that I was only enabling him. More rehab followed until our family was broke and in debt to the max and still no progress. I covered his debts, bailed him out of jail, and bought uniforms for the many jobs he attempted, only to fail. He was a Registered Nurse but when given the best jobs he only stole drugs to get high and lost those positions. He was such a good kid in most ways and brilliant in many. We watched as he spiraled down hill and there wasn't anything that we knew to do that would help him. In hindsight I now realize that the money we spent on rehab was money down a rat hole. The people running these establishments make promises that they cannot keep. I now realize that the parents must be the rehab facility with tough love. No money, no car, no freedoms. It was misplaced love on my part that enabled him to continue his drug use and all of the things I thought I was doing to help him were hurting him.

I lost my son and maybe it was inevitable but if I had it to do all over again I would be a different father. I would be unswerving in my saying NO to my son when he pleaded with me to give him money or a car. These are the avenues to finding and doing drugs. Now if he wanted to go to the store I would take him no matter how inconvenient it might be for me. If you love your addicted child, you must be the rehab. You must give your time no matter what. Then maybe, and only maybe, you will have a child who survives.

"D'you call life a bad job? Never! We've had our ups and downs, we've had our struggles, we've always been poor, but it's been worth it, ay, worth it a hundred times I say when I look 'round at my children."

W. Somerset Maugham, author

Thoughts from Joan
— Mother of Don

Don started smoking Marijuana, drinking and then onto Cocaine. Our family went through hell, all this through high school and after. Don went to jail for 6 months although not in the general population. He finally got into AA and is doing great.

Although this broke our hearts and no one can imagine what it is like sitting at a window talking to your child on a phone, crazy as this sounds jail was the best thing that could have happened to him. Our son came out clean and sober and has been to this day. The wonderful boy that we knew walked out of that jail a completely different person. I can't tell you how proud we are of him.

Jim and I feel mostly the same. Everyone is different but with us we were always there for Don and tried to help in every way. Now we know the parent has to step back and let it run the course. There's nothing a parent can do otherwise. The child has to want it bad enough to take control of their own life. Be there and love them always but don't make the mistake of enabling them in their addiction.

"It is easy to get a thousand prescriptions but hard to get one single remedy."

Chinese Proverb

"He who conceals his grief finds no remedy for it."

Turkish Proverb

Thoughts from Jim
— Father of Don

The best thing for the parent to do is to sit and talk with their child honestly. Like with myself the kids knew all about my addiction; what I felt inside, the guilt, remorse, loneliness and just a total empty shell. The alcohol gave me the feeling of worth but all the time I knew that the alcohol lied to me as will drugs.

Mainly drugs and alcohol have one job and that is to kill you! From what I hear and see every day - it is working well. Without my child getting into the program he wouldn't have a day being clean and sober because you can't do it by yourself.

I alone can never beat alcohol but together we can, and that is what I would tell any parent. You have to sit and talk to that child conversing back and forth, giving the proper advice in their situation.

"Romance fails us and so do friendships, but the relationship of parent and child, less noisy than all the others, remains indelible and indestructible, the strongest on earth."

Theodore Reik, psychoanalyst

"Loving a child doesn't mean giving in to all his whims;
to love him is to bring out the best in him,
to teach him to love what is difficult."

Nadia Boulanger, French conductor,
teacher of musical composition.

More Thoughts from Linda* — Mother of Jake*

*(*names changed to protect their privacy)*

WHAT PARENTS CAN SAY TO OTHER PARENTS: WATCH OUT!

Know that there are no guarantees in life and even the best efforts sour. But at least if your kid gets hooked and ruins their life or even dies, you will know that you did everything you could—encourage them to find their mission in life; develop their likes and talents; live life to the fullest, get an education—and so on…but should your child turn to drugs, if you've provided a functioning home, whether you as a parent are single or married, to the same sex or the opposite sex, it is not the doing of the parent.

If we parents cannot cure it (as Al-Anon tells us), if we are not powerful by our love and prayers, to cure them or catapult them into permanent recovery, then logic says, we didn't cause it, either!

Most likely the child carried the addiction gene, as scientists say exists in some brains by heredity, and often, there is some underlying mental or mood disorder, learning disability, or super or hypersensitivity to the pain of living that prompts the need for illicit relief and abuse of drugs. Perhaps the parts of the brain that govern self esteem or fear or pain, is not developed or working properly.

Support local and national government in passing bills into law to provide health coverage for mental illness and drug addiction and urge congressional representatives and senators to encourage tax support of scientific research into lifesaving treatments of addiction and mental illnesses that often underlie and prompt addiction (self-medicating).

Watch out for sleepovers at friends' houses!

Especially be suspect if your teen or young adult is sleeping all day in his/her bedroom on weekends or days off from work—consistently—and coming out only to eat a meal.

Watch out for the Denial Act: the teen or young adult who comes home and shares with you everyone he/she knows who has a drug problem—(OMG, you should have seen so-and-so…he's in a bad way…." and goes on to describe the awful facial color, the talking to oneself and delusional behavior, the disheveled clothes, in detail. Your child could be hiding or diverting your attention and giving the subtle message, "I'm OK. You don't have to worry about me." Start looking even closer, no matter how close you were with your child already.

The 'signs' of a drug addict are not always blatantly obvious. Maybe your son/daughter isn't red-eyed or stumbling in the door or acting anti social or violent. These are the hardest for parents to detect. We are often the last to know because we want so, to believe our child when he/she says, "don't worry, I don't do drugs."

Urine tests are not always reliable. Your child may be getting someone else's clean urine to present to you. Cold urines are a dead give-away it is not your child's. Kids also know about Golden Seal and other herbs to mask drug use in the urine and eye drops to mask red eyes. Rehabs are wise to the fake penises (Wizzinators for purchase on the web) to evade drug use, especially when monitored and mandated to rehab by the law. Do not sign for any packages delivered to the house, that you suspect might be unsavory.

Warn your kid not to MIX different drugs and/or alcohol. Most of the kids who die from drugs do not die from an overdose of one drug, but from a multiplicity of intoxicating substances that 'gang up' on the body and shut it down abruptly. **MIXING IS FATAL!**

Warn your son/daughter not to carry bags for others in foreign countries or sneak drugs into another country. The penalties are severe and they may never get out to go home.

The body is most vulnerable to death by overdose immediately upon release from rehab. Any prolonged time away from drugs, the body is not used to it, and may give out.

If your son/daughter starts unusually LOUD snoring in their sleep, check in on them and get help. Call 911.

If you suspect your son or daughter is a drug user or know that he/she is, keep naltrexone in the house, hidden. That is a chemical used in emergency rooms to reverse the effects of the drug and bring the person out of the semi coma (check this out).

If your child is being treated by a psychiatrist for mental illnesses, ask for a signed release from your teen or young adult over 18.

Talk with the psychiatrist as to the medicines they are prescribing and which ones can lead to abuse and addiction. Most psychiatrists have heavy patient loads and only spend 15 minutes with your child. Ask questions. Curb the amounts of anti- anxiety meds, especially, because they are highly addictive (Klonopin, etc.)

Monitor the amounts your child is taking. Look at the amount left in the bottles. Insist on having those bottles kept out of their bedrooms and in safe places only you know.

Write to government officials to have blood tests for drugs a mandatory part of medical physical examinations by physicians for kids ages 11 and over. They are more reliable than urines not watched as given.

Ask teachers to report any changes in behaviors, attention, grades.

Educate teachers to be aware and on the lookout for possible drug abuse.

Insist that schools monitor their grounds in between periods. That means having teachers randomly spot check rest rooms in between class periods, as well, and even during class. Those teachers who are free during certain periods, can also make a practice of sticking their heads inside the school bathrooms and making their presence known so it is harder for kids who might be using.

Finally - When your own child, no matter his/her age, wants to change his or her consciousness and be somewhere else and loves that altered realm over life itself and sooner or later, self-destructs, the pain of the survivors is beyond description. Bad enough one loses a child. Granted, the loss is profoundly injurious, a lifelong wound, no matter the cause, but when one has a hand in one's own demise, it is the antithesis of what a parent is supposed to be.

"According to data from the 2005 National Household Survey on Drug Use and Health (NSDUH) --
112 million Americans age 12 or older (46% of the population) reported illicit drug use at least once in their lifetime
14% reported use of a drug within the past year
8% reported use of a drug within the past month.
Data from the 2005 survey showed that marijuana and cocaine use is the most prevalent among persons age 18 to 25."

US Department of Justice
Bureau of Justice Statistics

Thoughts from Edith — Mother of Dennis and Grandmom of Anthony (Dennis's son)

With so many parents working outside the home, TV and Video games have become a part time babysitter. I'm guilty of that myself. I'll turn on TV as I cook, nap, send him upstairs if I want to watch something. They pick up so much from that. How do you think Miley Cyrus became so popular? No one reads Tiger Beat or 16 Magazine anymore. Anthony has picked up a lot of silly expressions, an extended-beyond-his-years vocabulary, knows the words to every song, all from TV or Video. For the most part it's a plus, but some things are too violent; the shows have an age in the corner but how many people look at those? I've seen shows about teen pregnancy, homelessness, gay issues and this is on Nickelodeon. At night it goes to a teen format from kids, so if a 6 year-old is watching it suddenly goes from ages 2 to 10 to 12 and up around 7 pm.

No one on ANY Channel ever has a drug issue on ANY show that I've watched for any age of kids. Even the soap operas show young kids shooting, having abortions, but no one in Port Charles, Llanview, or anywhere else has a drug problem. They make video tapes to teach kids to stay away from strangers, brush their teeth, be mannerly, but nothing about Pot, or any other form of drug.

Anthony got a wristband back in September or October with a bookmark for Drug Awareness Week, "Say No to Drugs," but no literature! Something else to rant about; You can become pregnant at any age in Pennsylvania and receive Welfare benefits, but if you apply for benefits because you're a drug user, you have to go to a doctor and have him fill out a form stating how long this will be a medical problem and keep you out of work and that's how long you receive benefits. I was so dumb about things that the doctor stated that in 9 months, Dennis would be able to function and go back to work. So I set a date to that. I wanted to know from Dennis why he wasn't

CURED? How dumb was I? And they stop your benefits on that date, unless you can prove you're going to meetings, and still in need of care. No one knows or cares about this drug problem, and sad to say, it probably won't get much better in our lifetime. It's so frustrating. As long as it's not in their face who cares?

"Parents need to fill a child's bucket of self-esteem so high that the rest of the world can't poke enough holes to drain it dry."

Alvin Price

Thoughts from Madonna — Mother of Shauna

I wished I would have been more aware of what the signs of addiction were. All those times she said she had a touch of the flu....I wish I had known it was withdrawals. Too little. Too late. I would most definitely advise parents to educate themselves on drugs; the signs and addiction. Educate like a life depends on it, because one may! I would tell kids to look at the other addicts during their down times and ask themselves, "Is that what I want to do with my life? Do they really look that happy?"

I feel like such a failure. I know it's not my fault and I did all I could, but still that endless pain in my heart tells me otherwise. I know, I know…

I told Shauna about drugs and alcohol and addiction. From the time she was a little girl, I talked to her and her brother about them and the temptation out there. I tried to educate her with what little I knew at the time. Her father is an alcoholic. I would point out his mood swings etc. Not in a negative way, but as an example. Scaring doesn't seem to help anymore, but maybe seeing someone....well we know that doesn't always work either. I just don't know.

I guess "Just say no!" Keep with that! That has to be the only way! Drugs are not cool they are deadly!!! Don't believe what other kids tell you! They want others to share their misery!

Maybe recovering addicts and we parents who have lost someone can be more involved in our local school drug and alcohol programs. We know what the results are.
But the main advice I would give is this....if it doesn't seem right, it probably isn't. You all know what normal is for your child. I'm not talking mood swings from hormones either. Parents need to investigate!

"Methadone Kills As Prescribed"

Sign seen at a HARMD protest on Capitol Hill in Washington, DC, 2008

Thoughts from Dorothy — Mother of Christopher

What Children Say....... this was said to me by my boy CHRISTO-PHER in the very, very beginning of his addiction to drugs..."MOM....I wish I can feel like I feel when I drink everyday." Now in the beginning I did not look into this because when I discussed this comment with my family the response was, "Oh, he is only going through a stage, or he is fine or he looks good or all kids drink; not knowing that THIS was the beginning of a bad thing.

My advice is to look at everything, not just the TEXT BOOK LIST but the hidden little things that can be passed off as the following:

1. SPOILED
2. LAZY
3. DOES NOT LISTEN

These are some of the other signs of addiction but in the early stages, I believe even before "THEY PICK UP."

I hope this will be a help to someone... this is what I saw in my life with my boy CHRISTOPHER, and this is what I wish I would have known...

"The whole of life is but a moment of time. It is our duty, therefore to use it, not to misuse it."

Plutarch, Greek historian, essayist

Heroin

"Heroin is a highly addictive drug, and its abuse has repercussions that extend far beyond the individual user. The medical and social consequences of drug abuse - HIV/AIDS, tuberculosis, fetal effects, crime, violence, and disruptions in family, workplace, and educational environments - have a devastating impact on society and cost billions of dollars each year.

Although heroin abuse has trended downward during the past several years, its prevalence is still higher than in the early 1990s. These relatively high rates of abuse, especially among school-age youth, and the glamorization of heroin in music and films make it imperative that the public has the latest scientific information on this topic. Heroin also is increasing in purity and decreasing in price, which makes it an attractive option for young people.

Like many other chronic diseases, addiction can be treated. Fortunately, the availability of treatments to manage opiate addiction and the promise from research of new and effective behavioral and pharmacological therapies provides hope for individuals who suffer from addiction and for those around them. For example, buprenorphine, approved by the Food and Drug Administration (FDA) in 2002, provides a less addictive alternative to methadone maintenance, reduces cravings with only mild withdrawal symptoms, and can be prescribed in the privacy of a doctor's office."

Nora D. Volkow, MD
NIDA   (National Institute On Drug Abuse)

THOUGHTS FROM PAULA — MOTHER OF ADAM

Seek counseling; tough love, addiction experts, marriage, family & individual. Your lives will turn inside out, upside down and your lives will be changed. Limit your time mourning the changes and gain strength by knowledge and support. Do not play the blame game or second guess yourself. The best piece of advice that I received was to stop trying to understand it - it is what it is. Is it nature, nurture, combo of both?-no answers, so save yourself the heartache and accept that fact real fast.

We had a family "intervention" and went through several rehabs with our addicted son. Another piece of advice: you can want, wish, guilt, threaten, cajole etc. the addicted person to stop, only they can do the work or recovery themselves. You must do your own work to learn how not to enable and how to survive while creating a new chapter to your family dynamics.

---

*"Dost thou love life? Then do not squander time,
for that is the stuff life is made of."*

Benjamin Franklin

Drinking cough medicine to get high.

Dextromethorphan (DXM)is the ingredient in cough syrup that causes the "high."

Dextromethorphan is a safe and effective active ingredient found in many nonprescription cough syrups, tablets, and gel caps. When used according to medicine label directions, the ingredient dextromethorphan produces few side effects and has a long history of safety. When abused in large amounts, it can produce a "high" feeling as well as a number of dangerous side effects.

Slang terms for dextromethorpha

Slang terms for dextromethorphan vary by product and region. Adults should be familiar with the most common terms, which include Dex, DXM, Robo, Skittles, Syrup, Triple-C, and Tussin. Terms for using dextromethorphan include: Robo-tripping, and Skittling, among others.

(www.drugfree.org)

ADVICE AND COMMENTS FOR CHILDREN

The following pages contain advice, and insight from the parents who have lived through this hellish nightmare of watching our child (or children) become helplessly and hopelessly ensnared by the Addiction Monster. We are not scientists, nor physicians offering opinions from a scientific or medical background.

We are parents! It's that simple. We're parents who have lived a life that none of us ever envisioned. We've had experiences that no one ever foretold us could happen. Did you ever think it could happen to you? Even if you thought it possible, did you ever really believe that it would happen? Did you ever truly consider that you might lose control of your child to the point of no return? Did you ever truly consider that you could lose your child, period?

How did that sweet, happy baby go from total dependence on us, to the teen years where they had all the answers and we parents were idiots and an embarrassment to them, which is a given in most cases, to crossing the line of normal rebellious teen behavior to the dark, deadly world of drugs?

As with all parents, we had no special training in how to raise a child. We did what came naturally as generations of parents have done before us.

It goes without saying that parents have always encountered difficulties and obstacles (I'm sure the parents in the 60s and 70s would attest to this) in raising a child. Consider this: "What is happening to our young people? They disrespect their elders, they disobey their parents. They ignore the law. They riot in the streets inflamed with wild notions. Their morals are decaying. What is to become of them?" Allegedly Plato quoting Socrates! There is some disagreement with who actually said this but the general consensus is that it goes back to the ancient Greeks.

Yes, children have always caused us elders problems but we accept their behavior, for the most part, as a part of their passage from babyhood to adulthood.

However, as Bob Dylan sang in the 60s, "The Times They Are A'Changin." Indeed they are. The enemies to our children's youth and insouciance are more formidable today.

Drugs have invaded our culture and society with all the force of a Category 5 hurricane. There seems to be no shelter from the devastating destruction that is taking our children down by the thousands each year.

What can we do? We wish we had all the answers. Unfortunately, no one does. But read the advice and thoughts from the following parents; advice that has been hard come by; advice that we truly hope will help you. It is never easy to say no to our children, but No just might be the biggest weapon you have in your arsenal against The Addiction Monster.

He lives long that lives well; and time misspent is not lived but lost."

Thomas Fuller

ADVICE FROM KAREN — MOTHER OF GINO

What advice do I have for children to help them say NO to drugs?

Children need to learn that drugs and experimentation can affect the rest of their lives. I would tell them that the younger they are when they experiment with drugs, the greater odds they have of becoming an addict.

I would also explain the genetic factor involved in families. It's been proven that addiction has a huge genetic factor to it.

Just saying NO isn't enough. Us as parents have been saying No for generations and the drugs are rampant.

Kids today need to know WHY they need to resist temptation and what the health risks are for them.

Now kids are abusing prescription medications.

As Parents we need to lock our medications up so they can't get into our kids' hands.

Don't assume your child wouldn't touch them. Why TEMPT them?

"Grief makes one hour ten."

William Shakespeare, author, poet

GHB

"Since about 1990, GHB (gamma hydroxybutyrate) has been used in the U.S. for its euphoric, sedative, and anabolic (body building) effects. It is a central nervous system depressant that was widely available over-the-counter in health food stores during the 1980s and until 1992. It was purchased largely by body builders to aid in fat reduction and muscle building. Street names include "liquid ecstasy," "soap," "easy lay," "vita-G," and "Georgia homeboy."

Coma and seizures can occur following use of GHB. Combining use with other drugs such as alcohol can result in nausea and breathing difficulties. GHB may also produce withdrawal effects, including insomnia, anxiety, tremors, and sweating. GHB and two of its precursors, gamma butyrolactone (GBL) and 1,4 butanediol (BD), have been involved in poisonings, overdoses, date rapes, and deaths."

NIDA (NATIONAL INSTITUTE ON DRUG ABUSE)

Thoughts from Angie
— Mother of Michael

Kids, read this and remember it! This could happen to you and your friends. We never thought it would happen to our child and his friends but it did. Don't let it happen to you or your friends.

Two weeks ago Em's friend Taylor passed away from what was first believed to be a heroin OD. Turns out it was Oxy! Same thing my Michael took.

Michael's best friend, Bryan, was at Taylor's house literally one week before and Taylor and roommates were all doing lines and lines and lines of Oxy. Bryan tried to tell him about Michael and how it would be the death of him if he didn't quit NOW. Taylor goes into detail about how he "had a system" and he's been fine for 8 more days.

One week later Bryan was standing at Taylor's funeral. Some system! This was at the same funeral home as Michael's, same cemetery, same reasons.

Bryan came over this weekend distraught over it all and how Taylor blew him off. Come to fine out, Taylor's roommates found him Sunday early morning. They called friends to come help destroy "evidence" and clean the house. They cleaned it completely and THEN called 911…while Taylor laid in his room, alone…and no longer here.

The police then called Taylor's mom and dad to ID his body. The same so-called friends spoke at Taylor's funeral. His poor parents are clueless.

"Did you know America ranks the lowest in education but the highest in drug use? It's nice to be number one, but we can fix that. All we need to do is start the war on education. If it's anywhere near as successful as our war on drugs, in no time we'll all be hooked on phonics."

Leighann Lord, Comedian, actress

Prescription drug abuse is a significant emerging problem in the United States

Most commonly abused classes of prescription drugs are:

Opioids, such as OxyContin and Vicodin, which are most often prescribed to treat pain; Central nervous system (CNS) depressants, such as Valium and Xanax, which are used to treat anxiety and sleep disorders; and Stimulants, which are prescribed to treat certain sleep disorders and attention deficit hyperactivity disorder (ADHD), and include drugs such as Ritalin and Adderall.

Risks of prescription drug abuse
Opioids:
 High risk for addiction and overdose. This is a major concern, particularly for recently synthesized slow release formulations, which abusers override by crushing the pills and injecting or snorting the contents, heightening their risk for respiratory depression and death.
 Dangerous combination effects. Combining opioids with other drugs, including alcohol, can intensify respiratory distress.
 Heightened HIV risk. Injecting opioids increases the risk of HIV and other infectious diseases through use of unsterile or shared equipment.

CNS Depressants:
 Addiction and withdrawal dangers. These drugs can be highly addictive and, in chronic users,
discontinuing them absent a physician's guidance can bring about severe withdrawal symptoms that must
be properly managed by a medical professional.

Risk of overdose. Overdose can cause severe breathing problems and lead to death, especially when
these drugs are combined with other medications or alcohol.

Stimulants:
Reputation as performance enhancers. Incorrectly perceived as safe for enhancing academic
achievement and weight loss, these drugs are highly addictive and potentially harmful.
Range of risky health consequence

NIDA (NATIONAL INSTITUTE ON DRUG ABUSE)

"To be in your children's memories tomorrow, you have to be in their lives today."

Anonymous

Advice from Linda*
— Mother of Jake*

(*names changed to protect their privacy)

WHAT PARENTS CAN SAY TO TEENS AND YOUNG ADULTS

Drugs are like Russian roulette. You never know which one of you carries the addiction gene that hooks you mercilessly into a downward spiral and life of doom…as evidenced by the (number in thousands) of deaths each year from prescription pills; cocaine; heroin; crystal meth, and so on, in the US alone.

Take pains not to mix alcohol with drugs. Be careful you do not mix several different drugs at once or over a period of several hours. It will surely kill you, maybe not this time, but the next, when the body's biorhythms may not be as resistant to the slowdown of vital organs such as heart and lungs. Without them working, there is no life. And you'll never know if that day is a 'bad day' for you because you will slip into a coma and die.

Once you get hooked, you'll be chasing the memory of that first high, for it will be a ghost. That ghost will never return to you. It will always just elude you, until you trip and fall and die. Addicts report there never is that same high again and so you will chase after something that doesn't exist and in that attempt to recapture it, you will fall deeper and deeper into a coma until death do you part—from everyone you know and love. You will have thrown your life away and cannot be revived or retrieved.

Drugs are evil. They make you do things you'd never do in your right mind. And drugs will never put you in your right mind. You will cheat, lie, sneak, steal—even kill—just to chase a high that no longer exists because your body is used to the drugs.

Drug addiction is a terminal illness. Do whatever you can, to treat yourself and recover. Go to rehabs and 12 step programs. Most are free in your community. Almost every town in America has a 12 step program, such as AA or NA. Ask your doctor for opiate blockers, if appropriate to your addiction. Ask your doctor for the cocaine vaccine when it comes out.

Remember, some recover from comas only to be lifelong paraplegics in vegetative states, or walking zombies wearing adult diapers.

You will need more and more drugs and will mix all sorts of substances in one sitting or over a period of several hours. Often, the mix of heroin or pills with cocaine and methadone (often abused on the street), will cause the heart grave confusion—up, down, around, until it gives up and you die. Addicts tend to get carried away once that hook is implanted, once that desire is sealed in cement and steel in the disordered brain, to get that first high back, that rush that betrays ever after.

Do what you must—change schools, go live with relatives somewhere else—until you can tame your demons that compel you to quest for the high that no longer exists.

Do not place yourself in situations that promote drugs—unsavory neighborhoods, questionable characters, nightclubs that give off a bad vibe, school yards at night…
Get home by 2am the latest, even if you're 18 or older.

Your parents and siblings and friends and relatives who all love you dearly, will never be the same. You will take them down with you, dead or alive, when you do drugs.

You can never bring back anyone you might kill while under the influence of drugs and alcohol with your car. Of course you won't realize you are too high to drive while under any substance's influence. You will not be in your right mind. You might as well be declared insane.

That pain will live with you the rest of your life, long after you have paid a lawyer, or hefty fine, or jail time. You will also have a criminal record which will hamper your finding a job. In having this occur, society might as well say it has little use for you.

You are already dead if you do drugs. Addicted to drugs, you are soulless and goal-less. You are a wretched shell of who you were and might as well be dead, not because your parents or teachers or anyone says so. You just have to look in the mirror. Once you start with drugs, you don't need any scolding or screaming at you. Drugs deem you your own judge, jury and executioner.

You may beat the odds and survive into your 30s and 40s but eventually the stuff catches up with you. Your physical and mental health is the first to go if you are 'lucky' enough not to die earlier on.

Drugs are lies in chemical form.
Drugs cause drug addiction.
Drug addiction is a psychic cancer that spreads and gets worse until you need and want more and more drugs, start overdosing or mixing different poisons and then you die.
Drugs are a false god.
Drugs sap all the life from their hosts until hosts become empty shells.
Then you die.
And decay in the ground.

We parents who love and guide you dearly, cannot always be around you. There are going to be times when they can't be there and you and you alone will have to decide your safety and make decisions that will make or break your well being.

Youth is a dangerous time in these times and in all times, but they can be beautiful if you take care of yourself and protect yourself from the harm of drugs.

You are responsible for yourself. If you get sick with addiction, it is ultimately your own responsibility to get well. You and you alone have to avoid temptation. Your family can support and cheer you on, but ultimately you must make it to the home plate of recovery. Just as a diabetic has to care and be committed to his/her own bodily care, so does the addict. Both are equally as ill.

Since recovery is hard and fraught with setbacks and relapses and 'triggers' that you think make you return to abusing substances, and with each relapse you risk death, it is far easier to not start using drugs at all, and avoid this dangerous spiral downward to destruction, altogether.

The law of nature is simple: survival of the fittest. Period.
You cannot survive drugs. One way or another, they will kill you.

If you know anyone addicted, pray for them that they come to their senses, that they get the medical and psychological care they need, the support of groups, the opiate blockers and work with all of these weapons to get off the drugs. Tell their parents, even though you know it is the most upsetting awful thing they can face about their teens or young adult children.

Be smart--don't start.

And tell your friends, be smart, don't start and that you will not hang around with them or get into a car with them when they are using.
The late twenties to mid thirties, seems to be the age where these kids die. I used to think drugs were a teen thing and they got out of it. I think we are the first generation of parents to see this phenomena happening...grown kids dying. The disease always had to be with humanity of course, but for some reason, it's as if it's a new disease.
 We as a society have got to find a way first to stop blaming the addicted one for the disease. But how do we do this while acknowledging that the person himself has to fight off the disease? We don't tell people with cancer to do this, do we? There are so many baffling elements of addiction disease...

"You have power over your mind – not outside events. Realize this, and you will find strength."

Marcus Aurelius, Roman emperor

Advice from Sherry
— Mother of Scott

The best advice I can give is to understand that drug addicted people are the most creative (although not really very good) liars!

A person under the influence of what I call The Addiction Monster will look you square in the eyes and tell you that night is day. He/she can steal your VCR, be carrying it out of the house and still tell you that is not what they're doing. If it were not so profoundly sad, their lies would be laughable. They're not.

The drug addicted person, however, believes that you can't see through them. They must truly believe they're pulling the wool over our eyes. This is how irrational the drugs have made them.

No matter what story your child has concocted, go with your gut instinct. A common ploy to wheedle money out of parents is to claim they owe money to a drug dealer and if they don't pay the dealer, unimaginable consequences will occur...anything from having their house/apartment burned down to their pets being killed and any number of threats they can think of. (They know what buttons to push to elicit the desired results**).**

I will share a horribly embarrassing personal story with you, just to illustrate how naïve we parents can be and the measures we will take to try to save our child's life.

To try to make my son aware that I would know if he was stealing from us, (something that he would have never done before drugs overtook him) I told him that I had sixty dollars in a jar that only he and I would know about. I told him that if the money turned up missing, then I would know for sure that he was stealing from me and there would be no way for him to get around it.

You're way ahead of me on this story already, I'm sure. Perhaps you're a lot smarter than me. But I sincerely felt that he would not want to destroy any faith I had in him and that this was a chance for him to prove his trustworthiness.

Ha! The money was probably gone that week but I didn't discover it until later because (oh no, she's not really that stupid is she?) I stopped checking after the first few days when it was still in the jar. How cunning of him. How incredibly trusting (and yes, stupid), of me.

So I would advise everyone to keep track of their possessions at all times. Keep money and anything of value in a lockbox and chain it to something so that it can't be transported out of the house.

Keep your car keys in a secure location so they can't steal your keys and go off in the middle of the night while you're sleeping. Check your car hood in the morning to see if it's hot.

Also be wary of so-called friends of your child, coming to your house telling you that your son/daughter borrowed money from them and they need it back. There's a good chance that the friend is in cahoots with your own child or he/she is trying to con you out of money to buy drugs for himself/herself.

If your child lives on their own and comes to you for money for food, for pet food, for medicine, whatever the reason, do not give them the money. But do offer to take them to the store to purchase these goods or purchase them for them. Whatever you do, do not put money into their hands. If you do, and your child is addicted, you are just buying their drugs for them!

Check your child's internet use! Drugs are easily purchased online.

Love your children with all your heart, always. But don't love them to death.

Comments from Jack — Father of Scott

They'll tell you that they lent their car to someone when in reality they've given it to a drug dealer for a specified amount of time in exchange for drugs. This is an incredibly stupid thing for the addicted person to do because the dealer using the car could be involved in a crime or wreck the car and this will all fall back on the shoulders of the addicted person. But addicted people don't think like "normal" people. They, in fact, are not even thinking. It's the drugs, or the Addiction Monster if you will, who is doing all the thinking; thinking about how to get money to get high, to feel "normal" again, to stop the hurting, the inner turmoil, the emotional pain, the anguish, the guilt.

The police are very wise to the practice of "lending" cars to drug dealers. We were even laughed at when we reported our son's car missing to the police. In the beginning of our son's drug use we were like babes in the woods. We believed his lies because previous to this downward spiral into the maelstrom of drugs and deception, we had no reason not to believe him.

Don't expect any sympathy from your local police department. To them your child is "just another addict." To hospital personnel who encounter emergency situations every day, the addicted person's overdose is quite often looked on with disgust.

Yet addicted people are sick too, very sick. Some have dual diagnoses of drug addiction and mental illness. They are punished throughout their lives for mistakes made in their youth. Addiction is not a life-style choice. It's a severe life-threatening consequence of youthful indiscretion.

"All of nature offers lessons on living, free of charge. One morning I noticed a dead tree supporting many living things--fungus, vines, lichen--which taught me that even after death we can continue to support those who live on. Living trees on our property teach other lessons. One tree has grown around a barbed wire fence. Another has grown around a nail, and a third through a chain link fence. These trees teach me how to accept irritation, absorb the pain and grow around problems. Nature teaches me how to find my place, grow toward the sunlight and bypass obstacles. To survive, we must be able to change in response to whatever is required by the challenge of the moment. Our bodies know this, but our minds often rebel when change is necessary."

Bernie Siegel, MD

Advice from Alice
— Mother of Danny

Watch your spoons!

Yeah I kept saying to myself where are all my spoons going to. It's not like they went out on the stoop in the summer, ate a Marino's water ice and then started digging in the dirt and lost my spoons.

I've found very creative bongs and what not, soda cans, plastic bottle and toilet paper rolls. Also hiding spots, in clothes pockets, in shoes, inside light switch covers, drop ceilings, under wall to wall carpet, see if it has been tampered with. Look under lamps, trophies, stuffed animals, etc. They are creative with hiding spots too.

"Dope never helped anybody sing better or play music better or do anything better. All dope can do for you is kill you — and kill you the long, slow, hard way."

Billie Holiday

MARIJUANA

"Marijuana is a green, brown, or gray mixture of dried, shredded leaves, stems, seeds, and flowers of the hemp plant (Cannabis sativa). Cannabis is a term that refers to marijuana and other drugs made from the same plant. Other forms of cannabis include sinsemilla, hashish, and hash oil. All forms of cannabis are mind-altering (psychoactive) drugs...

The main active chemical in marijuana is THC (delta-9-tetrahydrocannabinol). Short-term effects of marijuana use include problems with memory and learning, distorted perception, difficulty in thinking and problem solving, loss of coordination, increased heart rate, and anxiety."

Office of National Drug Control Policy

Comments from Lisa
— Mother of Ryan

My son Ryan started smoking marijuana the summer before starting middle school (around age 12, he's now 19). He was immediately hooked. No matter what I did or said, I couldn't get him to stop. I worked closely with the school officials even having him assigned a para-professional who went with him from class to class so he couldn't leave the building. Being the resourceful kid he was, more often than not I would get a phone call that he had managed to elude the kind man who needless to say quit after only one semester.

 Right after his 14th birthday Ryan experimented with "mushrooms" (I did not find out until over a year later). I woke up one morning and found him on the couch moaning. He had a high fever, was severely dehydrated, with body aches, cold sweats, and all the symptoms of the flu, only it wasn't flu season. I rushed him to the doctor. They couldn't find any infections in his blood or urine and determined he must have picked up a virus. It was 10 days before he was well again. Throughout the whole time I was telling him, "this is what you get for sharing joints with people, you never know what they have, etc." hoping this would scare him enough to stop. Well I was so proud of myself (for a year anyway) because Ryan stopped smoking pot!

A little over a year later I accidentally found out about the mushrooms by overhearing a conversation. I sat down with Ryan and asked him to tell me what happened. He admitted trying the mushrooms. He said within 5 minutes he felt a strange sensation throughout his entire body and couldn't see. His friends (with the exception of one) thought it was funny! Ryan wanted to smoke pot hoping it would calm him down. This one kid told him that he was having a bad trip and that if he smoked pot he would die. Luckily Ryan believed him. Sadly that same kid died from a drug overdose 4 months later. Ryan was devastated by his death. On the day Ryan told me what happened, he also told me that Dominick saved his life. He was

Ryan's angel even before he earned his wings.

To date Ryan remains pot free (but of course I still worry). He says he has never felt the same since his bad experience. There is nothing physically wrong with him but it did affect him mentally.

"Nothing is impossible; there are ways that lead to everything, and if we had sufficient will we should always have sufficient means. It is often merely for an excuse that we say things are impossible."

Francois La Rochefoucauld, French author

COMMENTS FROM PAM — WORDS FROM MARIA

Maria never said anything compelling about drugs. Her sarcasm led me to believe she would beat everything. Keep in mind, I NEVER saw her stoned on anything. She hid everything so well, that when I found her dying from heroin, with the beige foam coming out of her mouth, I thought she got drunk and was too lazy to wipe away her puke! I was even ready to put makeup on before leaving for the hospital because once I realized she overdosed, I thought she would pull through, and I was the one who said I'd lose her from the minute I found out about heroin, because the needle was always synonymous with death for me.

But I do remember one serious moment, after she had a few detoxes and was using again, when she said, "Don't worry, Mom, I am not having FUN. I haven't had FUN, and this hasn't been FUN, in a very long time!"

I am still blown away from my trip to Myrtle Beach last week where my husband's 23 year-old niece, who is still a heroin addict, on 5 years probation, a living zombie, who was raised with Maria, and even did heroin with her, came to visit with me at my hotel (she lives in Myrtle Beach with her mom now).

This girl, (who was my 6 year-old flower girl in my wedding to her uncle) is one of the most gorgeous creatures I have ever seen: blue eyes, blonde hair, tall, slim and curvy,
and showed me the black and blues on her breast from still shooting up in her breast, and gave me the news, that she now has Hep C.

As we all said in the past here, we want our kids back, but not addicted, and I am still reeling from seeing her. She was in jail when Maria passed, and when she got out 6 months later, I was the first she came to see. She visits me when in New York between relapses and jail time, so my head is just spinning right now.

> *"Nobody saves America by sniffing cocaine.*
> *Jiggling your knees blank-eyed in the rain, when it snows*
> *in your nose, you catch cold in your brain."*
>
> **Allen Ginsburg – American poet**

ADVICE FROM CELESTE — MOTHER OF BRANDON

This may be hard for kids to read but this is from a mother, probably much like your mom.

The pain of watching our children lose their way is a pain that never goes away. As parents we have such high hopes for you and our main concern is your happiness and safety.

While dealing with the anger and sadness, we often forget that your addiction has become a mental illness. No amount of fighting or trying to reason with you seems to help. Your introduction to drugs is the beginning of a long journey in and out of rehabs and a deep pain that we do not want to see you suffer through. You will suffer in more pain and self-loathing than you can imagine.

We love you so much we will become blind to your pain and so the yelling will begin. This will only end with your death and beginning of our lifetime of guilt. We will all feel we should have done more for you, tried harder. We will always be there for you, cry with you and we really do feel your pain.

Don't ever turn us away. We really are here to help. I don't know if my son understood how much he was loved and how many people he could have turned to. Maybe you are trying to save us from this but don't. We have to somehow make you understand that we know you are an addict or en route to becoming one and we need you to take down those walls and let us in. Only then, can we save you. If you have a friend in trouble, help them. Talk to anyone that can help them. Their lives are worth saving.

"New Study Indicates That People Who Experienced Prolonged Displacement from Their Homes after Hurricanes Katrina and Rita Had Higher Rates of Mental Health and Substance Abuse Problems.

"This report shows that most people are resilient – that they can overcome tremendous adversity," said SAMHSA Administrator Terry Cline, Ph.D. "But it also shows that when people are displaced from their homes it can be devastating, and that mental health resources can play a critical role in enabling them to fully recover from such a trauma."

SAMHSA
(Substance Abuse and Mental Health Services Administration)
– OFFICE OF APPLIED STUDIES

MORE THOUGHTS FROM PAULA — MOTHER OF ADAM

Advice for children not to start drugs: Advice to parents and children: First sign of usage go to therapy immediately. Seek places that will show you graphic materials of how people's lives change, what they look like, visit bereavement groups, cemeteries. Sounds extreme....extreme times call for extreme measures.

Parents: From day 1 you have modeled behaviors for your children. If you use, you are setting an example. If you associate with such your children will think that it is OK to associate with such.

Children: Your mind and body is a onetime gift. Treat it well. Diet, exercise, continue to educate yourself, read, explore, be spiritual, be thankful and grateful every day for your blessings, be charitable, and choose your peers wisely. Aspire and inspire vs. expire.

> *"Nothing can stop the man with the right mental attitude from achieving his goal; nothing on earth can help the man with the wrong mental attitude."*
>
> **Thomas Jefferson**

"Addiction should never be treated as a crime. It has to be treated as a health problem. We do not send alcoholics to jail in this country. Over 500,000 people are in our jails who are nonviolent drug users."

Ralph Nader, American activist and lawyer

ADVICE FOR DOCTORS FROM MAXINE — MOTHER OF LANG

The advice I have is for the DOCTORS mostly. Why would ER doctors repeatedly give a patient oxycodone (at the patient's request), for various aches and pains, (nothing serious) never checking the patient's chart to see that he never saw a primary care physician? The ER doctors were advised to FLAG the chart, DSB (drug seeking behavior). It was pointed out by the patient's own mother to no avail. They kept giving it to him.

Lang practically had a standing order for Oxycodone! He would go in and he would tell them what he "needed." I told the doctors over and over to look at his records (he had plenty of them) that he was seeking drugs, but they were too busy. They are given out too freely.

When a patient goes to hospitals away from home for drugs - DUH that should send a red flag too. There are too many signs that they chose to ignore. The doctors are "enablers" for sure.

"Sometimes doing the right thing hurts. But we should always do the right thing. Doing the wrong thing hurts even more."

Jack McGinnis, Science teacher, retired

"Keep steadily before you the fact that all true success depends at last upon yourself."

Theodore T. Hunger

More Thoughts From Pam — Mother of Maria

My advice to children or even adults ready to take that drink or try that drug is this: whatever your feelings, current circumstances, problems, or whatever pain you think you need to lessen, will be so minute compared to becoming an addict or alcoholic.

You will soon find out that every problem you thought you had was nothing compared to being addicted. When addiction and alcoholism cause you to be shunned by your community, unable to keep a job, considered untrustworthy by all in your orbit, and you are even able to feel and see the physical effects in the mirror, it will be too late to realize how truly insignificant all those "triggers" you thought you had truly are.

Addiction caused my daughter to lose all her self-esteem and she deemed herself a loser due to all the unforeseen repercussions which stemmed from her addiction.

Also, because she started using drugs at 14 with the "gateway" drug of cannabis, she was never able to grow up emotionally. Drug abuse retards emotional and psychological growth in terms of fully understanding consequences, and therefore time becomes devalued; there is no mature sense of immediacy to complete tasks, pass courses, and move ahead with life chronologically in a healthy manner.

Once an addict gets clean, there is the painful realization of all the time and opportunities that cannot be regained; hence the relapse, and the vicious cycle continues.

Pamela Palmer Mutino, author:
Swish: Maria in the Mourning

"Success is the sum of small efforts, repeated day in and day out."

Robert Collier

MORE THOUGHTS FROM MAXINE — MOTHER OF LANG

I would say the signs to look for in an addict are these:

A new group of friends you don't know. Group(s) of friends who stop by the house briefly (short visits), then disappear, a drop in grades if school age kids, lack of interest in grades, lack of interest in the usual passions, sleeping more or less than usual, phone calls from unknown people, trips to the emergency room for insignificant aches and pains, trips to nowhere (vague).

These are harder to control when the child is older or an adult. You cannot monitor them 24/7. Lying to you about anything and getting good at it. And last but NOT LEAST - things missing from your house.

As for what I told my child "just say no to drugs" means nothing once they are addicted. Just hope and pray that they never TRY drugs. He argued with me that marijuana was not addicting, that it was harmless. That may be true, but it leads to something "better," the truly addicting drugs.

My son never admitted that he was a drug addict. He always downplayed it. He always told me that he could handle it with God's help and with my help. But he lost on both accounts.

"Time is a physician which heals every grief."

Diphilus, Greek dramatist, poet

"I can honestly say all the bad things that ever happened to me were directly attributed to drugs and alcohol. I mean, I would never urinate at the Alamo at nine o'clock in the morning dressed in a woman's evening dress sober. "

Ozzie Osbourne – musician, singer

In Our Children's Words

On the following pages you will read words from our children reaching out with a very important message for your present and your future.

These same children did not want to become addicted. They did not want to cause grief and heartbreak to their parents. They did not want to cause the guilt, shame, and pain to themselves. They did not want to die!

If you are a teen or young adult reading this book, please heed the words of your peers, those who have struggled with addiction, and those who have lost their lives, but who might be able to help you save yours.

Be yourself. Listen to yourself. Be strong. Do what you know to be right. Choose friends who have the same values. Don't let others corrupt you.

The teen years are a mere blip on the radar screen of your life. Yes, these years can be very difficult, trying to fit in, to be popular and accepted by the "cool" kids (or whatever the current term is for the "in crowd" today). Don't let them dictate **your** future. This is your decision. Your entire future is at stake and you're the one who will be living it. Whether you live your life in peace and happiness or in jail or a juvenile center, are ultimately your decisions. Make the right one!

"I wanted a perfect ending. Now I've learned, the hard way, that some poems don't rhyme, and some stories don't have a clear beginning, middle, and end. Life is about not knowing, having to change, taking the moment and making the best of it, without knowing what's going to happen next. Delicious Ambiguity."

Gilda Radner, actress, comedian

Thoughts from Alice
— Words from Danny

The first thing that comes to my mind and probably will always stay with me forever is when Danny FINALLY asked me for help.

What stands out to me is while waiting 8 hours for a bed at detox, Danny asked for only two things; one was to not have to sit in the waiting room as it was too uncomfortable and he was so sick. He wanted to stay in my van and lay down in there. He asked me to park it right in a spot close to the doors and if I would keep going in they would know he did not leave and he would not lose his spot.

The second thing he asked was to use my cell phone to call his sister Alicia. He got on the phone with her and was sobbing. He begged and pleaded with her. He said "Alicia, I'm soooo sick. Please promise me you won't ever do drugs. Please stay away from anyone who does drugs. Once you start this it is so hard to stop. You don't want to end up like me. Promise me please. I love you, I'm sorry."

"You may have to fight a battle more than once to win it."

Margaret Thatcher, former UK Prime Minister

"It is a good rule to face difficulties at the time they arise and not allow them to increase unacknowledged".

Dr. Edward W. Ziegler, Presbyterian Minister

Angie's Thoughts — Michael's Words

Michael told me drugs were everywhere.

"EVERYWHERE mom. You can manage to eliminate one kid selling them, and there will be 5 others to take his place. No matter what circle I turn to, they are there. If I hang with the sober friends I feel like a loser and like I have no life. I miss my friends."

He would tell us many times he was sorry for all the trouble he got into. He would always be so remorseful after the fact. He told me he had no control. If he drank, he did it excessively. He could not just have a few beers and chill. If he smoked, he did it excessively. He worried himself sick about his sister and little brother getting involved. He called Emilee nightly to tell her to not do these things and if she did he would kick her butt. He knew the heartache it brought and how out of control he was with all of it.

He said they went into the school bathroom and put alcohol in their 7-ups during lunch. The main place all the pills came from — medicine cabinets of parents who never missed them. He constantly asked his girlfriend why she was with him. He never felt worthy of anyone's love.

> *"We may think there is willpower involved, but more likely…change is due to want power. Wanting the new addiction more than the old one. Wanting the new me in preference to the person I am now."*
>
> **George Sheehan, Physician, Author**

"Alcohol is a drug. It alters your mind, body and emotions. It is also our nation's largest youth drug problem, killing 6.5 times as many young people as all illicit drugs combined."

MarinInstitute.org

Words and advice from Stacey on My Space about Danny (Alice's son)

So many people lose their lives every day to the disease of addiction. It's not fair, I know. This illness will take your life without thinking twice. It's cunning and cruel. It cares about nothing, but yet we still let it get the best of ourselves. There is so much more to life, if you could just get past the beginning months without the use of heroin. Life is so much better than any high and people need to come to realize this.

Danny was so young and will never have the chance to be able to make a life for himself or have a family. He left behind a lot of loved ones. A lot of people were in his corner praying every day that he would realize and come through, a mother who is a wreck, who doesn't understand why. All she knows is that her son is no longer with her. It's her worst fear come to life. Don't let this be you. Learn from everyone who has passed away from this disease in the past. Use them as an example.

So when you're mourning the death of our dear friend, do it with a prayer and a new step in your life. Don't do it by going out and getting messed up because you think that's how he would want it. Because if he could tell you what he wanted I'm sure it would be that you learn from him and not make the same mistakes!

Dan wanted a better life and struggled every day. The best gift we could give is to "learn." Learn from other people's mistakes because once you make that wrong choice, sometimes we don't get the chance to change.

Remember heroin kills a lot of people every day. It's no joke. It will take your life right from under you. When will people learn? All we can do is be strong, face our fears and realize we don't need dope to live. Learn from all the people who sacrificed their lives. Your life is precious, and remember YOU ARE SOMEBODY!

I love you Danny, and I'm sorry you had to go out this way. It's no way to say goodbye to the world and leave the ones that we love. You'll always be in my heart and in my prayers. Until we meet again, I will miss you. I hope you will be there when times are tough. You can help show me the light.

Love and miss you always and forever,
Stacey

> *"Down, down, down into the darkness of the grave, gently they go, the beautiful, the tender, the kind; quietly they go, the intelligent, the witty, the brave. I know. But I do not approve. And I am not resigned."*
>
> **Edna St. Vincent Millay, poet**

Words and Thoughts from Madonna and Shauna

What did Shauna say? She said Mom, you'll never understand. I don't do heroin for the high, I do it to get rid of the sickness. (I don't believe that)

She also told me it's a feeling that is indescribable. She told me over and over she was self medicating, but she never knew why or what she was depressed from.

She told me she never believed those D.A.R.E. classes that told them one time and you're addicted. She believed it after her one time!

She told me she wished she could be normal. She told me she was sorry for everything she had done to me and that she loved me and always knew I loved her unconditionally. I did....and always will.

"Heroin is easier to get than alcohol. The liquor stores and bars eventually close but the heroin stores are open 24 hours a day."

JoinTogether.org

"With the shift in heroin abuse patterns comes an even more diverse group of users. In recent years, the availability of higher purity heroin (which is more suitable for inhalation) and the decreases in prices reported in many areas have increased the appeal of heroin for new users who are reluctant to inject. Heroin has also been appearing in more affluent communities."

NIDA (NATIONAL INSTITUTE ON DRUG ABUSE)

THOUGHTS FROM THERESE, WORDS FROM GREG

Therese: Greg has been clean since Jan 3, 2007. We have had our rough times. He's had a rough month. He hasn't slipped but he has been tempted. The one thing I have learned is that the road to recovery is so full of twists and turns. Their self esteem is so low that anytime they feel the hurt you have to be there.

Greg: During the past year, I have come to realize that life, as well as an addiction, is not that simple. One must realize the complexity of the times, recognize the needs and remember the love of family.

Realize that schools, society, and families have changed. Schools and families were once safe havens that nurtured all that was good in society. That safety net no longer exists. Schools, unfortunately, are pressed to achieve standardized goals that tax faculty to meet and exceed yearly goals. Families are no longer the dream families of the 70's that solve problems over the dinner table or on vacation.

By realizing that complexity, I have gained insight into the needs of my generation. We are losing far too many hurting hearts and souls. Recognize the need to listen. Recognize the need to dream. Recognize the importance of self respect — never allow someone to destroy your respect of self. You are special.

Recognize the need to be yourself. Never allow others to use you or question what you are. Remember the need to be you is much more important than the need to fit in.

Remember the love of family will always be true. Those strangers that allowed you to lose yourself are not family. Family will love, guide, and accept you. They will never leave or abandon.

"Today's students can put dope in their veins, or hope in their brains. If they can conceive it, and believe it, they can achieve it. They must know it is not their aptitude but their attitude that will determine their altitude."

Rev. Jesse Jackson, Minister, Civil Rights Leader

WORDS AND THOUGHTS FROM CELESTE AND BRANDON

Brandon suffered with his addiction for over 10 years. We all saw it but couldn't stop it. He once said "Mom, if I stay here, I'm gonna die." We sent him to Florida, away from his life here but the pull of drugs was strong and he lied to come back. Stated the court said he had to come back.

We sent him to live in California for a time. No luck there either. He said "There are more drugs here than home." Again we gave in and he came home.

He knew he'd die but often said "Whatever." He just didn't seem to care anymore. What horrible pain they must be in. After losing several friends to this, he called heroin users "stupid losers," only to die of the same. "It's the ******* pills" was his favorite out. Can't remember so can't be blamed. What logic. But to him it was logic.

Brandon was in and out of rehab for all these years. We sent him to boot camp for addicts in the Pocono Mountains. After 9 months of doing well he came home and within months was back on drugs.

We stood by him arrest after arrest, relapse after relapse. We watched our happy, bright boy become a sad young man. He never lost hope for recovery and we never lost hope of getting him back. We all lost in the end. He lost his life and we lost our Baby.

"We are what we repeatedly do. Excellence, therefore, is not an act but a habit."

Aristotle, Greek philosopher

LSD (lysergic acid diethylamide) "ACID"

"One of the strongest mood-changing drugs. It is sold as tablets, capsules, liquid, or on absorbent paper.

"Sensations and feelings change much more dramatically than the physical signs. The user may feel several different emotions at once or swing rapidly from one emotion to another. If taken in a large enough dose, the drug produces delusions and visual hallucinations. The user's sense of time and self changes. Sensations may seem to 'cross over,' giving the user the feeling of hearing colors and seeing sounds. These changes can be frightening and can cause panic."

"Most users of LSD voluntarily decrease or stop its use over time. LSD is not considered an addictive drug since it does not produce compulsive drug-seeking behavior, as do cocaine, amphetamine, heroin, alcohol, and nicotine. However, like many of the addictive drugs, LSD produces tolerance, so some users who take the drug repeatedly must take progressively higher doses to achieve the state of intoxication that they had previously achieved. This is an extremely dangerous practice, given the unpredictability of the drug."

NIDA (NATIONAL INSTITUTE ON DRUG ABUSE)

Thoughts from Brownie, Friend of Sandi's Daughter, Jennifer

Tell all the people who warned you, worried about you, or cared enough to tell you about your problem, and tell them that you are quitting. Everyone thinks that by concealing it, no embarrassment will befall them because no one will know. But, they already do! For every one person that has told you about your problem, there are 10 people that talk about it behind your back.

Then, call the people you use the drug with, and tell them you can't hang out with them anymore. You will lose all but maybe one of these friends. If there is one friend of these you have left, tell him/her they can't bring the drug over when you two hang out. This eliminates temptation and possible sabotage.

For every 1 person who wants to see you clean, 10 people don't. They want the hook-up or they want someone to share the drug with. With them, it's not "how are you doing?" it's more "how much you got on you?" And, about one of these people feels that if they share this habit with you, they can get you sexually. These are the hardest to stay away from because there's a part of you that wants to have sex with them or have a relationship with them, without realizing they are keeping you addicted. You can't have anything to do with them until you are clean, yourself. More than likely, by the time you are clean, they will have moved on to another. By the time you are clean, you won't want them anyway.

If you do not hope, you will not find what is beyond your hopes."

St. Clement of Alexandra

"Everything one does in life, even love, occurs in an express train racing toward death. To smoke opium is to get out of the train while it is still moving. It is to concern oneself with something other than life or death."

**Jean Cocteau, French poet, novelist, actor,
film director and painter**

Thoughts from Paula —
A word from her son Adam

An addict speaks out: My son, a handsome, witty, intelligent, sensitive and talented young man started with alcohol at age 13 and moved onto drugs shortly thereafter and died at the tender age of 24 from an overdose. He was not happy, he was addicted. He could not sleep well, live well, cried, so saddened and one time said to me, his mother; "I wish that I never started with the stuff."

"What in the world ever became of sweet Jane? She lost her sparkle, you know she isn't the same. Livin' on reds, vitamin C, and cocaine. All a friend can say is 'Ain't it a shame?'"

"Truckin'" by the Grateful Dead

When asked where would he be now if not for Drug Court,
"I think I would be back in the courtroom
– except in shackles."

Diego R. (Drug Court Graduate)

THOUGHTS FROM BARB – MOTHER OF BRENT

Brent had moved back in with me five months before he died. He had been homeless for a month and I talked him into moving back with me. I figured I could help him get on his feet. Boy was I wrong!

He did well for the first two months and into the third month and then the addiction really kicked in and he was worse than ever with his using.

With my parents help, my husband and I staged an intervention. It was successful in the respect that he went into treatment, but he walked after three days.

He came back to my house and within a few weeks had a horrific car accident with a company vehicle and was fired from his job.

He was using 24/7 so on the advice of a professional addiction doctor I gave him an ultimatum. My husband and I sat him on our couch and said "You either go back into treatment or you leave."

This is what he said: "This is my life, not yours. I like getting high and drinking and I am not going to stop. It is not a glamorous life, it has highs and lows but they are *my* highs and lows.

I said "Even if it kills you?" He paused for awhile and gathered his thoughts and said "I am not afraid to die."

I asked him to leave my home and he did.

Exactly one week later he was found dead.

How very, very sad.

Author's Note: Barb Smith and her husband, Tim, have started the "I Took A Stand" campaign which you can watch on You Tube. Here is more information from Barb who, along with her husband Tim, is dedicating her life to helping children enjoy a drug-free life.

I Took A Stand Campaign

My name is Barb Smith. My 23 year old son Brent died Dec. 4, 2005 from the consequences of a drug and alcohol addiction.

Since the death of my son I have been compelled to tell anyone who will listen about the dangers of using and abusing drugs and alcohol.

One year after his death God laid it on my heart to write a book about Brent's struggles called Brent's World. The book was published in Oct. 2007 and has been a success.

In February of 2008 God laid it on my heart to start a drug and alcohol prevention program at my church called "I Took A Stand." My husband Tim and I kicked the program off with a video shoot in March of 2008. We taped the young people taking a stand and pledging not to use drugs or alcohol. We have followed up the video taping with weekly 1 hour meetings where we discuss drugs, peer pressure and anything else the young people would like to talk about. We also have basketball events where we take the young people to the park to play basketball and eat pizza. We are trying to show them they can have fun without using drugs or alcohol.

The program has been a huge success and I feel we are really reaching the young people.

The program is very simple and can be rolled out anywhere and with any age group. If you are interested in learning more about the program you can contact me through my website (www.compassionhearts.com)

I am willing to share the program with anyone at no cost.

THOUGHTS FROM JAN – MOTHER OF CINDY

Tonight I was thinking of contributing something to your book and just couldn't get into it. Suddenly it was stirring up old memories of addiction and I couldn't go there. My most important point I would like to tell parents and children is that it is a myth that addicts have to hit bottom before they will turn around. If they have hit bottom it is too late and they may not make it to turn around. A friend of Cindy's told me addiction was like walking into the forest. You go in and then can't find your way out. You get deeper and deeper into trouble.

Here is something I found in Cindy's papers. We don't know who the author is but we appreciate these words.

POSITIVELY NEGATIVE

We drank for happiness and became unhappy

We drank for joy and became miserable

We drank for sociability and became argumentative

We drank for sophistication and became obnoxious

We drank for friendship and made enemies

We drank for sleep and awakened without rest

We drank for strength and felt weak

We drank medicinally and acquired health problems

We drank for relaxation and got the shakes

We drank for courage and became afraid

We drank for confidence and became doubtful

We drank to ease our conscience and felt greater guilt

We drank to make conversation easier and slurred our speech

We drank to feel heavenly and ended up feeling like hell

We drank to forget and were forever haunted

We drank for freedom and became slaves

We drank to erase problems and saw them multiply

We drank to cope with life and invited death.

Author unknown

"I see that a man cannot give himself up to drinking without being miserable one-half his days and mad the other . . . "

Anne Bronte, author

THOUGHTS FROM CHRIS – MOTHER OF BRETT

If there was one thing I was sure of in life it is that I taught my children, through example, that drugs and alcohol have no value or place in this world. I was so sure of myself that I had taught that lesson well that I did the unthinkable...I let my guard down.

For the last 12 years I have even been out speaking about the dangers of substance abuse and bringing heart wrenching stories to kids and that increased my comfort zone. My kids knew my platform, as I shared many of the stories with them and I believed it was enough...that we were SAFE. On Father's Day June 19, 2005 my safety net....which already had a few holes in it, finally disintegrated....with the death of my 22-year-old son, Brett. How could this happen to me? What did I do wrong...how could he not have heard my message....felt my fear....or known how it would destroy me to lose him?

Just before his death I learned that his older brother was using drugs....I even witnessed a psychotic episode...and it rocked my world to the core. Everything I believed I had accomplished in my role as a mother vanished. All that felt safe and normal disappeared into gut wrenching heartache and a feeling of disillusionment that was life changing.

It took only four months for my son's accidental addiction to pain killers for them to end his life. He was a personal trainer...had just signed up for fire school...and he wanted to LIVE. He was desperate to get off the speeding train he was on...I believe knowing that it would end in his death. I believe he had heard all that I tried to teach him...and felt powerless to stop the collision course he was on. At times, I try to imagine his fear...his desperation…and it crushes me in a torrent of tears and sadness.

While I have always believed that things happen for a reason....the death of a child can never be reasoned with...but I try. You see, since I have been out there speaking for 12 years....the addition of Brett's story is very powerful. The kids see me as a normal mom...they hear the random stories, then the one about the young man I mentored who died on my birthday of a drug overdose in 1999. When I put on the t-shirt with Brett's picture...and play the DVD of his life....there is not a dry eye in the room. I ask the kids to sign my son's website...and many do...each one thanking me profusely for opening their eyes. It helps to know I might be saving other children from the same fate...but it does not ease my pain or dry my tears. It is the least I can do....to preserve his memory and to know that maybe, just maybe, a child will be tempted and stop to remember how touched they were when I crossed their path. What else do I have left to cling to but that hope?

"Junk is the ideal product...the ultimate merchandise. No sales talk necessary. The client will crawl through a sewer and beg to buy."

William S. Burroughs, Author

The Killer Lurking in your Medicine Cabinet

(Prescription Drug Misuse)

By Larry Golbum, R.Ph., MBA
The Prescription Addiction Radio Show - Breaking the Silence
(www.prescriptionaddictionradio.com)

The Prescription Addiction Radio Show – Breaking the Silence exemplifies the power we each have as individuals: As a pharmacist, beginning in December 2003, I had the ability to find out where the prescription drugs on the streets were coming from that dramatically affected my family. It was in January 2004 I filed a complaint with the Florida Medical Board about the doctor who was distributing the drugs "via prescriptions." It wasn't until April 2006 a final decision was made by the Medical Board. The Administrative Complaint before the Medical Board displayed that the doctor distributed over 9000 addictive drugs to a drug addict over a fourteen month period. Many of those drugs ended up in the wrong hands in Pinellas County. After I waited 27 months, the Florida Medical Board simply fined the doctor on a Saturday morning and allowed him to continue his drug distribution on the following Monday. I still remain outraged by that decision. Drug dealers spend years in jail for dealing and selling much fewer pills.

I admittedly was waiting for some severe discipline from the Florida Medical Board, and the board members who we put our trust in to protect the citizens simply took a few bucks from the doctor and told him "to be more careful." That doctor still distributes narcotic prescriptions as I write this.

There is a small 1000 watt radio station in Clearwater, Florida. I did not know that at night the signal could barely be heard five miles from the station. During the daylight hours, I heard a commercial that said: "you too can be on the radio." I found out that for $125 I could buy an hour on the radio. I had never, in my life, been on the radio. Anger can make you do foolish things.

I spent three weeks writing my first script and spent one hour on the radio on a Sunday night on October 22, 2006. A "divine" force has continued to create a radio program every Sunday night since. It wasn't until February of 2007 I had a web site. It was rudimentary, but the visits started coming. I did not have a professional web site until the following August. I moved to a much larger signal the following October that would broadcast to the entire Tampa Bay area of Florida. The growth of the radio show has been slow, but steady.

I will forever be appreciative that Novus Medical Detox became my first sponsor in March of 2008. Every week more people find out about the show and the visits to the web site continue to increase. We are all spokes in the wheel at bringing a greater awareness of the growth and dangers of what I term "the new opium epidemic in our country not seen since the introduction of heroin over 100 years ago". My goal from the beginning was to create a program that can be used as a tool for every person and group who realizes, or has been affected by, the silent epidemic that is growing in our country. I am pleased and flattered that Sheryl McGinnis has found the radio show to be worthy of both her trust and judgment.

The medicine cabinet has become the symbol of our modern day war on drugs. It was the introduction of Oxycontin in late 1995 that appears to have been the impetus for the ever increasing reports on prescription drug misuse in recent years.

In the early 20th century, our country learned first hand of the dangers of heroin yet almost 100 years later the FDA allowed a drug on the market called Oxycontin that can duplicate the effects of heroin. The drug companies have been ingenious at marketing and selling the entire class of opioid related drugs to an unwitting public who still thinks that "prescription" means "probably safe."

The miracle drugs of penicillin, diabetes, high blood pressure, asthma, HIV and a myriad of additional classes of drugs are truly representative of the wonders of modern pharmaceutical research. However, the opium plant has been with us for at least 5000 years, morphine for over 200 years and heroin for over 100 years.

The drug companies have masterfully marketed and placed the opioids into the mindset of modern medicine. The promises of pain relief from the same molecular entities used in the Civil War almost 150 years ago have turned into a nightmare of death and addiction for way too many families. We have almost an entire medical profession who has not connected the twisted science the drug companies are presenting with the reality of the negative outcomes being reported regularly from the opioid related drugs.

We are bombarded with advertising and information to lock up our medicine cabinets. The message is that your medicine cabinet contains drugs that are dangerous for your children and does not mention the dangers lurking for adults in that same cabinet. The reality of the statistics reveals more people over 35 are dying from those drugs in the medicine cabinet than children.

The drugs in the medicine cabinet are not marketed or sold with the children in mind. The drugs in the medicine cabinet are manufactured, sold, prescribed and distributed to the unsuspecting adult who has been convinced that the danger of the pills only lies in the wrong hands of our children. The morgues and addiction treatment facilities are the recipients of all the people who have had their hands in the family medicine cabinet.

Abuse vs. Misuse — A Very Important Distinction

Prescription Drug "Abuse" – The Semantics Have Become Important

Addiction, overdoses and death all fall under the umbrella of "abuse".

The term abuse has been skillfully created by the powers who can then absolve themselves of all responsibilities from the dangers that too many prescription drugs possess. The drug companies continue to promote and sell as much product that they possibly can that continues to have outcomes that do not match up with the promises of the science being presented.

The present statistics indicate that 70% of all related drug deaths have prescription drugs involved. The press and media always report that the death was due to "abuse." The outcome of addiction from taking the narcotics that are marketed as "painkillers" (termed "junk" on the street) is due to "abuse." The alprazolam implicated in a death is called an "anti-anxiety" medication. On the streets alprazolam is sold as "ladders, totem poles and bars".

The doctor who prescribed the drugs and the pharmacist who dispensed the dangerous products, after many years of education, have no responsibility for a negative outcome. That term "abuse" protects everyone involved with the distribution of the products. The courts hold the drug dealer on the street corner liable, but the drug dealers in the white coats remain beyond reproach.

It is time the term "misuse" replaced "abuse." Misuse refers to the misinformation and hidden information the drug companies are slow to reveal. Misuse refers to the doctors who don't understand the dangers of the drugs they are dispensing. Misuse refers to the pharmacists who willfully complete the drug deal with little understanding of why they are handing out drugs that are killing and addicting people. And, misuse covers the unfortunate event that too many times takes place once in the recipient's hands.

The term misuse implies that everyone who is part of the poor judgment in the over marketing and over distribution of too many addictive pills should be held accountable. We have millions of people who cannot get through their day without chills, shakes, diarrhea and tremors if they do not get their addictive prescription drug in them. Most people are taking the drugs exactly as prescribed by their doctor, some even in death. The term "misuse" is an appropriate definition and the term "abuse" is insulting to the people who continue to be affected every day.

I do hope the media begins to report on the ingenious method that the drug companies and medical professions have skillfully promoted by using one word to sway the mind set that it is ALWAYS the personal responsibility and fault of the individual who is affected by the misuse of the drugs regardless of the number of accomplices involved in a negative outcome.

"Prescription narcotic drugs are of the most used and abused medicines. In 2002 almost 30 million people (almost 13% of the population 12 and older) in the United States had used prescription pain relievers non-medically in their lifetime."

(www.streetdrugs.org)

"*Listen to the Exhortation of the Dawn!*
Look to this Day!
For it is Life, the very Life of Life.
In its brief course lie all the
Verities and Realities of your Existence.
The Bliss of Growth,
The Glory of Action,
The Splendor of Beauty;
For Yesterday is but a Dream,
And To-morrow is only a Vision;
But To-day well lived makes
Every Yesterday a Dream of Happiness,
And every Tomorrow a Vision of Hope.
Look well therefore to this Day!
Such is the Salutation of the Dawn!"

Kalidasa, Indian poet and dramatist - c.170 BC

An Interview
with Eric Nestler, MD, Ph.D.,
UT Southwestern Medical Center

Eric Nestler, MD, Ph.D, UT Southwestern Medical Center Professor of Psychiatry and Neuroscience received his BA in molecular biophysics and Biochemistry from Yale and his medical degree from Yale University in 1983 and did his residency at Harvard Medical School in Medicine and Psychiatry.

His professional associations include the American College of Neuropsychopharmacology, American Society for Biochemistry and Molecular Biology among others.

The Eric J. Nestler Laboratory of Molecular Psychiatry - The University Of Texas Southwestern Medical Center at Dallas states on their web page:

"The goal of the laboratory of molecular psychiatry research is to better understand the ways in which the brain responds to repeated perturbations, under normal and pathological conditions. A major focus of the research is drug addiction: to identify molecular changes that drugs of abuse produce in the brain to cause addiction, and to characterize the genetic and environmental factors that determine individual differences in the ability of the drugs to produce these change. Similar work is underway in the areas of depression and stress."

"The improved insight into the neurobiological mechanisms of addiction and depression that results from our research will guide future efforts toward the development of more effective treatments for these disorders."

Dr. Nestler, your credentials are impressive to say the least. We're honored that you have taken the time to address the issues of drug/cocaine addiction with us which is of great concern to

many of the people reading this book.

Q: Do you think scientists and/or researchers such as yourself might one day be able to make the brain "forget" how good the drugs make them feel, thereby causing them to not do them again? Would this be a viable form of treatment?

A: It's conceivable. I really don't know how likely.

Q: Are "triggers" physical, psychological or a combination of both? What is the most effective thing addicted people can do to avoid these triggers?

A: Triggers are mostly psychological, I think, but mediated via chemical changes in the brain. The best approach is to "extinguish" the triggers, in other words, for someone to be exposed to the triggers repeatedly to relearn they mean nothing.

Q: Do you think there is a chance there will be some form of aversion therapy that will make the addicted person turn FROM drugs, to eschew them knowing that they might have some physical effects (vomiting/diarrhea for example) if they take drugs (such as Antabuse does for alcoholics)?

A: In general, our experience with Antabuse tells us that this will not work for most people.

Q: Is it true that people who start taking drugs while in their teens for example, remain at that level emotionally throughout their life? Just as smoking supposedly stunts physical growth, does taking drugs stunt emotional growth?

A: No, I don't think this happens. But the younger a person is exposed to drugs, the more likely it is they will become addicted.

Q: We've heard there is a cocaine vaccine in the very near future. Is there any truth to this, and if so, do you hold much hope for its success?

A: The vaccine is in development and may be ready for clinical use soon (within a year or two). Whether it will work or not remains unknown. I'm skeptical, because even if it blocks the effects of cocaine, it won't work against cocaine-like drugs (amphetamine, methamphetamine) and most addicts will find those other drugs.

Q: Does a person, who has been addicted for a long time, say from their teens into their late twenties, have a chance for the brain to return to normal? Or will that part of the brain that causes the cravings, remain, perhaps dormant such as the varicella (chicken pox) virus (shingles in adult life) remains in a person's body?

A: There is every evidence that the brain will recover, but it could take years.

Q: Is there truly an addiction gene? I've read that Chinese researchers have discovered many genes responsible for addiction. Can someone be born with the addiction gene that predisposes them to addiction?

A: There are likely numerous addiction genes. However, unlike genes for eye color and height, or for some diseases like Huntington disease, which produce their effects in all cases, genes for addiction (like genes for adult onset diabetes, most cancers, high blood pressure, etc.) cause the illness only under some circumstances. That is, addiction genes make some people more vulnerable so that when they're exposed to drugs they're more likely to get addicted than other people.

Q: How much does nature vs. nurture come into play when talking about cocaine addiction?

A: As above. The idea is that certain people are born with genes that make them vulnerable to addiction. However, if all goes well, less stress, less peer pressure, less exposure to drugs, strong parental oversight, etc., etc., etc., they may do fine. Likewise, a person with a relatively low innate vulnerability, if exposed to many stresses, may still become addicted.

Q: When a parent first discovers their child is doing cocaine, should immediate psychological counseling be instituted along with rehab?

A: Yes. Parents have to be aggressive. They need to find out why the kid is using drugs, which may be as simple as peer pressure to being under too much stress, to having some other emotional problem (depression). The treatment would vary accordingly.

Q: I've been told that the recidivism rate for heroin addicted people is 98%. Would this hold true for people addicted to cocaine? And if so, what good are rehabs? Most rehabs are only for a very brief time, 3 to 4 weeks yet cost the families thousands and thousands of dollars.

A: The recidivism rate for most addictions is 80% within 6 months of the end of treatment. The key is to keep trying, failure after failure. Eventually most people do find a way out if they can stay safe in the meantime. The hope is to develop a medication that would make psychosocial rehab more effective.

There has unfortunately not been sufficient progress in treating cocaine addiction. There remains no FDA approved medication treatment for example and non-medication approaches (psychotherapy, rehab, etc.) are inadequately effective in most people. The hope would be that some medication, to be developed in the future, will then make psychosocial rehab (which will always be needed) much more effective.

We have learned a great deal about the neurobiological mechanisms underlying cocaine addiction and this work has provided ideas for developing new treatments. Most of these ideas are still in development. It can take 20 years before an idea is adequately tested in people. This of course is unacceptably slow for the patients and families involved, but it reflects:

a) the complexity of the brain, b) the difficulty in making a fundamentally new type of medicine that is safe and effective, and c) getting that medicine approved by the FDA. I do believe that we'll be seeing several new ideas tested over the next 5 years and the hope is that at least some of these ideas will prove true.

"The first and the best victory is to conquer self."

Plato, Greek philosopher

Interview with Florida State Representative Aaron Bean

Below is a brief interview with Florida State Representative Aaron Bean of District 12 in northeast Florida, including all or parts of Nassau, Baker, Bradford, Union, Clay and Duval counties.

Representative Bean was elected in 2000 and his term expires in 2008. He is currently Chairman of the House Healthcare Council which oversees all health legislation and spending for health, which is currently a $23.5 billion budget.

Representative Bean is a bank president in Fernandina Beach and is married with three sons.

Thank you Representative Bean for taking the time out of your busy schedule to answer our questions.

Q: I understand that New Jersey recently passed the Mental Health Parity Bill for Addictions – Substance and Alcohol. Will Florida be doing the same?

A: The Legislature did pass a version of Mental Health Parity this year that specifically outlines coverage for some types of mental illness. The concern with parity and other mandates is that it drives up the costs of health insurance that less people could end up with any coverage at all.

Q: Bill Janes, the Florida Drug Czar, is actively and passionately supporting a Florida Drug Monitoring Bill. We are only one of fifteen states that still have no legislation in place. Admittedly, some of the legislation is flawed in some states, but with all the knowledge and experience that exists concerning the data bases in other states, will you actively be supporting Bill Janes and Governor Crist next year to get effective legislation passed?

A: I am termed out after 8 years in November, but there is some great momentum towards a Drug monitoring. So many folks have called, emailed, sent a letter to me and my colleagues in the Legislature that it has moved the issue from the back burner to front and center. If this momentum continues, I am optimistic that the 2009 session could be the year.

Q: Why are so few politicians displaying the courage that you are by speaking out on such a devastating disease?

A: Most likely, unless you are personally affected by prescription drugs, you do not even know that there is a problem. I only became aware after speaking to friends and family who are pharmacists – that gave me a clue – that a major problem is out there.

Q: We consistently hear about how dangerous the drugs are for our children, but the facts are that most of the people dying with drugs in their bodies are over 35. How do we get the message out that the prescription drugs are dangerous for the adults as well?

A: Part of the bill could be a public awareness campaign. But the best way, I believe, is straight from the doctor's and pharmacist's mouth – that these drugs are addictive and dangerous.

Q: Privacy is always the prime concern when talking about the drug data base bill. With these dangerous drugs addicting and killing so many of our citizens, do you think people would be willing to accept the data base knowing it could save a child?

A: Privacy is an issue, but hopefully, with strict penalties for misuse and using modern technology to help protect privacy as much as possible, we could go forward with a database.

"The significance of a man is not in what he attains but in what he longs to attain."

Kahlil Gibran

Interview with Amelia Arria, Ph.D, Addiction Researcher

Dr. Arria, Thank you so much for the giving of your time and experience as an addiction researcher to try to help parents understand a little more about addiction and the tough job of parenting. Please share with our readers your background.

Dr. Arria: My name is Amelia Arria. My undergraduate work was in human development and family studies and I have a Ph.D. in epidemiology (public health).

For the past 15 years, I've conducted research in the area of addiction. The addiction field is very broad because it touches almost all aspects of living in our society – parenting, pregnancy, education, the legal and criminal justice system, the health care system - the list goes on.

I've had the chance to study many aspects of the problem, but most recently I have been focused on understanding how the problem of substance abuse develops in young people and ways of preventing the progression to addiction.

Who do you work for?

Dr. Arria: The University of Maryland College Park and the Treatment Research Institute in Philadelphia.

What kind of work do you do?

Dr. Arria: Research

What is the best advice you can give to parents on how to help their child be drug-free?

Dr. Arria: From the very start, parents must communicate with their children honestly and directly. They have to make sure children are safe and feel loved. They need to keep focused on guiding their children to use their talents, to fulfill their potential, and engage in healthy behaviors.

Parents need to be parents – they need to be empowered to make decisions about their children's lives that sometimes aren't understood or accepted easily by the child, but that the parent knows is in the child's best interest to keep them safe. Parents need to be aware that all children have unique characteristics and that one of the most challenging jobs a parent has is to figure out what kind of a child they have and what they need to succeed in this very complicated world.

As children grow older, especially during adolescence, the role of the parent gets even more challenging than when their child was younger. Exposure opportunities to alcohol, tobacco and illicit drugs only increases as children age, and parents have to keep informed and educated about the contexts in which substances are used, the reasons why adolescents use, and how to respond when their child begins to use. Through monitoring and supervising activities as children age, as well as communicating disapproval of any substance use clearly and unambiguously, parents are key in delaying the onset of drug use.

Finally, parents need to realize that underage drinking and tobacco use are not only harmful for their child's development in several ways, but also linked to later substance use problems, and thus should not be condoned or encouraged in any way.

Do you have any further comments on how substance abuse develops and ways of preventing the progression to addiction?

Dr. Arria: It's such a huge question - maybe it is important that the progression is very different depending on the individual and their environment. One of the hallmark signs of trouble is continuing to use despite problems. The key to prevention is assessing the signs early and intervening as soon as possible - and not brushing things off as a "rite of passage" - one of my least favorite sayings when it comes to alcohol and drug use.

I'm working with the Partnership For A Drug Free America on a number of tools for parents that we hope will help them navigate these challenges.

"Enablers" in the world of substance abusers

By Heiko Ganzer, LCSW-R, CASAC, CH

The purpose of this article is to help family members understand the concepts of "enabling" and "helping" when living with addiction. In order to continue "using," the addict often needs and seeks others to assume their responsibilities and, through different cons, gets others to "care take" them. The article "I Am Your Disease" was written to illustrate some of the traps which cause addicts to relapse and become addicted. This article is written to the addict's close family or friends who may inadvertently "enable" while seemingly trying to help their addicted family member or friend. I also review how the nature of the addiction lends itself to such a conspiracy and include some points on effective addiction treatment and how it will be differentiated from other forms of treatment.

Defining enabling

According to the dictionary, the word "enabling" is defined as "empowering a person to do what they would otherwise be incapable of doing; to make possible, practical or easy." It is generally viewed as a positive word and the "enabler" is seen as a "helping" person. However, those who have been living with addicts have felt long ago that to "empower" the addict to do what he or she would otherwise be incapable of doing is not only *not* helpful—it can even be deadly. Thus, within the field of substance abuse the perception of an enabler has acquired its own definition: The enabler refers to a person (or even an institution) caught up in the process in such a way as to allow for the maintenance and downhill evolution of the disease of addiction.

With time, the substance abuser's existence starts revolving more and more around their drug of choice. They become preoccupied with efforts to control their use, as well as sheltering their supply of drugs. Sheltering may take the form of concealing use, keeping a supply continually available and hidden, arranging for absences, going only to parties where drugs are accepted, and so forth. As the substance abuser's dependence on drugs increases, so does their dependency on others (people). In order to continue using, the addict must somehow arrange to have their job and family responsibilities taken over by others. They need a constant supplier of money and a dealer. Addicts thus become notoriously effective in finding people to fill such needs.

The way in which the substance abuser gets others to help meet those needs can be quite subtle and it is not unusual for a family member or friend to become enmeshed in an interaction with a substance abuser which may appear superficially helpful but which actually may support the downhill progression of the disease of addiction. The enabler does so by removing painful consequences and by denying the addict the opportunity of assuming the responsibility for the consequences of their own behavior. In essence, the enabler joins the substance abuser in covering up and denying the problem. The substance abuser is thus allowed to become less and less responsible and free to continue use. The enabler acts so for myriad reasons—lack of knowledge about the disease, trying to be helpful, wanting to be liked, self-protection, and so forth. There are many good books written on co-dependency but my favorite writer on the subject is Melody Beattie (Co-dependency No More).

Thus, in the world of substance abuse the concept of an enabler has acquired its own definition: The enabler refers to a person (or even an institution) caught up in the patient's process in such a way as to allow for the continuation and downhill progression of the disease of addiction. The enabler acts so for numerous reasons:
- lack of knowledge about the disease
- trying to be helpful
- wanting to be liked
- self-protection
- trying to be kind and rescue

The enabler can be a friend, a family member, or a professional. For example, they may be the spouse of a substance abuser calling their partner's supervisor on Monday morning stating that once again their partner is sick and will be out for the day consequently covering up the real issue and avoiding the consequences and prolonging the ability of the addict to use their drugs.

Are you an enabler?

1. Have you ever "called in sick" for the substance abuser, lying about his symptoms?
2. Have you accepted part of the blame for his (or her) use or behavior?
3. Have you avoided talking about their substance abuse out of fear of his response?
4. Have you bailed him out of jail or paid for his legal fees?
5. Have you paid bills that they were supposed to have paid themselves?
6. Have you loaned them money?
7. Have you tried using drugs with them in hopes of strengthening the relationship?
8. Have you given them "one more chance" and then another and another?
9. Have you threatened to leave or throw them out and didn't?
10. Have you finished a job or project that the substance abuser failed to complete themself?

So what do you do?

First you can join wonderful self help organizations like "Alanon", "Coda", or "Gamanon." These helpful groups don't ask for money and operate on the "12 steps." They are easily found on the internet directory and are local. Second you should seek a qualified therapist; one who has qualifications in substance abuse (CASAC) and gambling problems. Third, is that other family members should be aware and provide support. If the addict does not wish to attend AA, NA, or Gamblers Anonymous then an interventionist should be called in to perform an intervention and assist the family in getting the addict the help they need.

Illegal drug use among teenagers is declining. However, the abuse of prescription drugs, especially pain relievers is increasing. Many teenagers assume that prescription drugs are safe, when in fact they are highly addictive and can cause severe side effects.

(www.teendrugabuse.us)

A History of Addiction
by Claudia Black, MSW, Ph.D.

The following chapter is a fascinating look into the origins of alcoholism, chemical dependency, addiction and addiction treatment encompassing such notables as Alexander the Great to Bill W., cofounder of Alcoholics Anonymous.

Below is Dr. Black's biography followed by her report – *History and Addiction*

Claudia Black, M.S.W., Ph.D. is a renowned author and trainer internationally recognized for her pioneering and contemporary work with family systems and addictive disorders. Since the 1970's Dr. Black's work has encompassed the impact of addiction on young and adult children. She has offered models of intervention and treatment related to family violence, multi-addictions, relapse, anger, depression and women's issues. Dr. Black designs and presents training workshops and seminars to professional audiences in the field of family service, mental health, addiction and correctional services.

Since 1998 she has been the primary Clinical Consultant of Addictive Disorders for The Meadows Institute and Treatment Center in Wickenburg, Arizona.

Dr. Black is the recipient of numerous national awards including the 2004 Distinguished Alumni Award from the University Of Washington School Of Social Work. Dr. Black has been a keynote speaker on Capitol Hill in Washington, D.C. and on Parliament Hill in Ottawa, Canada. Her workshops have been presented to an extraordinarily wide array of audiences including military academies, prison systems, medical schools, and extensive mental health and addiction programs. Claudia has extensive multi-cultural experiences working with agencies and audiences in Japan, Brazil, Australia, Scotland, Iceland, Germany, England and Canada. Many of her books and videos have been translated and published abroad.

Claudia is the author of *It Will Never Happen To Me* (two million copies sold), *Changing Course, My Dad Loves Me, My Dad Has A Disease, Repeat After Me II, It's Never Too Late To Have A Happy Childhood, Relapse Toolkit, A Hole in the Sidewalk, Depression Strategies, Straight Talk, The Stamp Game: A Game of Feelings,* and her latest *Family Strategies* and *Anger Strategies.* She has produced over twenty videos and several audio CDs.

Dr. Black received her Doctorate of Philosophy, Social Psychology, from Columbia Pacific University, 1983, Master of Social Work, University of Washington, 1977, and Bachelor of Arts, Social Welfare, University of Washington, 1973.

Like every aspect of mankind, addiction has its own history. Long before anyone understood the core problems of addiction, people became hooked on substances. The following is adapted from Dr. Claudia Black's videos – The History of Addiction and The Legacy of Addiction.

History and Addiction

Chemical dependency has plagued humankind since man first crushed grapes. Each millennium has treated the problems that addiction brings with a methodology unique to the times. Historically, society, as a way of treating those addicted, has imprisoned them, banished them, put them in mental institutions, religiously converted them and, in today's world, treated them. What has not changed is the impact of chemical dependency, particularly on those addicted and their families. Herein lies the story.

The roots of addiction are deep and ancient, and the methods used to deal with addicted persons are historically bizarre. The Egyptians used to flog drunkards; the Romans created Bacchus, a God of wine and revelry; and the Turks "cured" drunkenness by pouring molten lead down the throat of the inebriate, perhaps the first example of aversion conditioning – crude, but effective. The Greeks believed that the use of amethysts, beautiful deep purple stones, would ward off drunkenness. They festooned their cups with amethysts, wore them when drinking, and even ground them up and put them in the wine they drank.

An example of an early addict we might recognize is Alexander the Great, king of Macedonia in 350 B.C. By the age of 31, he had conquered the world and, during all his mighty triumphs, had abstained from intoxicating beverages. However, after his great triumphs, in a short span of two years, Alexander became an alcoholic and ended his career in a series of insane escapades. He burned cities at the request of a courtesan and killed his best friend, and his demise came in a contest of wine drinking. Alexander the Great was 33 years old when he drank himself to death.

Wine making and its export became the economic basis of the Roman Empire. With the collapse of the empire, religious institutions, particularly the monasteries, became the source of brewing and wine making techniques. It was not until the 19th century that the production of beer, wine and distilled beverages became efficient and cheap enough to supply inexpensive alcohol to the masses.

Throughout the 19th century and into the early 1900s, alcohol and various drugs – notably morphine, cocaine and chloral hydrate – were used in various combinations as medicines. These "patent" medicines were highly addictive; alcohol content was as high as 95 percent. By the mid-1800s, the problem of addiction was major and growing. A physician from Battle Creek, Michigan, traveled extensively and used charts to show the effects of alcohol, drugs and nicotine on the body. Today, you would most likely recognize him as the founder of Corn Flakes. His name was Dr. John Harvey Kellogg. In the 1840s, the first large temperance group, The Washingtonians, was born. The origin of this movement was a drinking club that met nightly at Chase Tavern in Baltimore, Maryland. One night, 20 chronic drinkers, in a spirit of jest, sent two of the younger members to a temperance lecture. Upon their return, the two men presented a favorable report of the lecture, and an argument concerning abstinence began. This argument would last four days and ended when six of the members announced their decision to support an abstinence society. This became a huge movement, with a membership of almost five million Americans by 1845 – notable because it probably marks the beginning of modern-day addiction recovery.

Like Alcoholics Anonymous, the Washingtonians believed in the substitution of personal experiences for lectures, and they viewed the drunk as a sick person. Perhaps most significant, they also professed a singleness of purpose; to help the drunk. But politics became an issue and would cause the movement's demise.

America's most recognizable temperance leader may be Carrie Nation. In 1888, she began a campaign wherein she and her female followers destroyed kegs of liquor and sometimes entire saloons, using stones and trusty hatchets.

In the late 1880s and early 1900s, some bizarre forms of addiction treatment were practiced. The Keeley Cure began in 1880. Using bichloride of gold, the treatment involved withdrawing the alcohol or narcotic drug and restoring the nerve cells to their original unpoisoned condition, thus removing the craving for liquor. Enemas and laxatives then stimulated the elimination of the accumulated poisonous products. (Incidentally, Bill Wilson, co-founder of Alcoholics Anonymous, was subject to this treatment in 1934). In 1918, it was stated that more than 400,000 people had been treated by this system at various Keeley Institutes. (NOTE: Bichloride of gold did not exist.)

While not concerned primarily with addiction, the Oxford Group, a popular religious movement in the 1930s, was to play an important role in the future treatment of the disease.

But perhaps the most successful treatment for alcoholism has been Alcoholics Anonymous. Dr. Bob Smith and Bill Wilson founded AA in 1935 in Akron, Ohio. Wilson was a drunk who, after being called on by an old friend and member of the Oxford Group, was admitted for his alcoholism to Towns Hospital in New York City in 1934. He remained sober, and his work took him to Akron, where he felt the need to talk to another alcoholic. He was introduced to Dr. Bob Smith, a prominent and persistent drunk. From this meeting emerged the basic premise of Alcoholics Anonymous; one alcoholic helping another alcoholic. The original meetings of Alcoholics Anonymous were held as adjuncts to the Oxford Group on Wednesday nights at Dr. Bob's house.

Alcoholics Anonymous is a spiritually based program, and its primer is The Big Book. Proposed names for the book were One Hundred Men, Moral Philosophy, The Empty Glass, The Dry Way, and Dry Frontiers. In 1939, 5000 copies were published. Today there are four editions of The Big Book – and millions and millions of copies. Alcoholics Anonymous exists in most countries, with meetings in just about every city in the world.

In 1950, Lois Wilson, wife of Bill Wilson, founded Al-Anon, the 12-Step program for families and friends of alcoholics. Alateen was started in 1957.

In 1951, the "Minnesota Model" was developed. The foundation for treatment from the 1970s to the present, this abstinence model is based on the 12 Steps of Alcoholics Anonymous. It has become the primary protocol for residential and outpatient treatment programs in the United States and in many parts of the world.

In 1952, the American Medical Association defined alcoholism, but it would not be until 1967 that it passed a resolution identifying alcoholism as a complex disease and recognizing that the diagnosis and treatment of alcoholism are medicine's responsibility. While abstinence-based programs would become widespread throughout the United States, treatment in the late 1970s would focus on all chemicals, not just alcohol. The word "alcoholism" was gradually replaced by "chemical dependency." There would be a resurgence of interest in attending to the family, spouses, partners and children of addicted persons. There also would be heightened interest in both young and adult children of alcoholics.

The role of the private sector in treatment has lessened, with community-based programs taking on more responsibility. Today's recovery programs treat addictive disorders, recognizing cross-addictions and the need to abstain from all mind-changing chemicals. In many cases, clients are treated for multiple addictive disorders, such as gambling, chemical dependency, eating and sexual disorders, and dual diagnoses, most commonly PTSD and affective disorders.

Addiction is a complex disease, a devastating disease and a terminal disease – yet today it is a treatable disease. History has left us a long and painful legacy of addiction. Today we are beginning a new legacy: that of the reality of recovery.

Appeared in the 2006 Spring MeadowLark

The author is most appreciative of Dr. Black's contribution to this book. For further information you may contact Dr. Black at her website (**www.claudiablack.com**)

WHAT SIGNS SHOULD I LOOK FOR IF I SUSPECT MY CHILD IS USING DRUGS?

TIPS FROM PARENTS (AND THE AMERICAN COUNCIL FOR DRUG EDUCATION)

EMOTIONAL SIGNS

*It is important to note that some or several of these signs may very well be just the behavior of typical adolescence. Our advice to you is to know your child and go with your gut instinct. It's best to err on the side of caution. Don't be in denial.

Increased appetite especially for sweets
Falling asleep, nodding off, while in the middle of eating
Change in overall attitude/personality with no other identifiable cause
Changes in friends; new hang-outs; sudden avoidance of old crowd; doesn't want to talk about new friends; friends are known drug users
Doesn't want to bring new friends home
Doesn't want to give last names for new friends
Vague about where he/she met the new friends
Change in activities or hobbies
Drop in grades at school or performance at work; skips school or is late for school.
Change in habits at home; loss of interest in family and family activities
Difficulty in paying attention; forgetfulness

General lack of motivation, energy, self-esteem, "I don't care" attitude

Deep sleep punctuated by loud snoring, difficulty waking up

Sudden oversensitivity, temper tantrums, or resentful behavior

Moodiness, irritability, or nervousness

Silliness or giddiness

Paranoia

Excessive need for privacy; unreachable

Secretive or suspicious behavior

Car accidents

Chronic dishonesty

Unexplained need for money, stealing money or items.

Change in personal grooming habits

Possession of drug-related paraphernalia such as pipes, rolling papers or small decongestant bottles, metal, copper and stainless steel scrubbers (one popular brand is Chore Boy) used as a filter in a crack pipe

Small clear tubes which can be purchased at convenience stores (usually with a rose on it) to be used in smoking crack in conjunction with the Chore Boy or other such abrasives

Beer or soda cans compressed in the middle with a hole in them, used for smoking crack

Memory lapses, short attention span, difficulty in concentration

Poor physical coordination, slurred or incoherent speech

Unhealthy appearance, indifference to hygiene and grooming

Bloodshot eyes and dilated pupils - often find them using eye drops in their eyes

Possession of drugs, peculiar plants, butts, seeds or leaves in ashtrays or in clothing pockets

Makeup on inside of arms purportedly to cover up "bruises" but in fact may be used to cover up needle tracks

Drug-related magazines, slogans on clothing and posters

Conversations and jokes that are preoccupied with drugs

Hostility in discussing drugs

Music which glorifies drugs

Odor of drugs, smell of incense or other "cover up" scents

PHYSICAL SIGNS

Loss of appetite, increase in appetite, any changes in eating habits, unexplained weight loss or gain
Slowed or staggering walk; poor physical coordination
Inability to sleep, awake at unusual times, unusual laziness
Red, watery eyes, pupils larger or smaller than usual; blank stare
Cold, sweaty palms, shaking hands
Puffy face, blushing or paleness
Smell of substance on breath, body or clothes
Extreme hyperactivity; excessive talkativeness
Runny nose, hacking cough
Needle marks on lower arm, leg or bottom of feet
Nausea, vomiting or excessive sweating
Tremors or shakes of hands, feet or head
Irregular heartbeat

If your son/daughter starts unusually LOUD snoring in their sleep, check in on them and get help. Call 911
Linda — mother of Jake

The main advice I would give is this....if it doesn't seem right, it probably isn't. You all know what normal is for your child. I'm not talking mood swings from hormones either. Parents need to investigate!
Madonna —mother of Shawna

Lying about anything and everything is one of the biggest clues of drug use along with evasiveness. New friends who call the house and come over to visit but stay only a couple of minutes (usually because they are either buying drugs from your child or selling drugs to your child). The same goes with phone calls, a quick conversation and your child hangs up the phone and then goes into his bedroom (perhaps waiting for a drug dealer friend to come by his/her bedroom window) or after the phone call, your child suddenly has to go out somewhere. This can happen more than once in a night.

Not being where they're supposed to be and unreachable by phone and giving lame excuses as to what happened. Go with your gut instinct.
Sherry — mother of Scott

Change in behavior, habits, communication, missing household items (either used for their "kit" or used to finance their addiction). Trust your instincts, if it seems to be off - It is.
Paula – Mother of Adam

"Hold yourself responsible for a higher standard than anyone else expects of you. Never excuse yourself."

Henry Ward Beecher

INTERVENTION

WHAT YOU SHOULD KNOW

(Courtesy of the Partnership For A Drug-Free America) www. drug-free.org

Many of you may be aware of the A&E TV series "Intervention" which is a weekly television show. We weren't aware of interventions when our own son was struggling with his addiction. Would an intervention have helped? We just don't know and it only adds to our stress to contemplate the What Ifs.

Below is a reprint on Intervention from the Partnership For A Drug-Free America. It tells you all you need to know about interventions, how to perform one, what you should do. It is a very informative guide that we wish we had known about. I'm pretty sure we would have tried it. We left no stone unturned while trying to help our son. Unfortunately we didn't know about this stone. Perhaps an Intervention is the right thing for your family. Read on.

The Partnership For a Drug-Free America Intervention Quick Guide

The word "intervention" is commonly misunderstood. Our Intervention Quick Guide was created to help clarify the term intervention- and to offer information on how to go about conducting one.

So, what is an "Intervention"?

Talking to the person you're concerned about is called an

"intervention." There are two types of interventions – informal and formal.

An informal intervention means having a personal discussion with the person you're concerned about. This could be as simple as asking a few questions or making a couple of observations.

A formal intervention means having a structured conversation with the person. This involves bringing together a group of people with the substance user to explore how his or her use has affected all their lives. The formal intervention is usually used when the person has repeatedly refused to get help.

The point of any intervention is to ask the person to take concrete steps to address the problem and lead them to the help they need (i.e. go for an evaluation, attend counseling, enter in- or out-patient treatment.)

The key thing is not to wait for your loved one to "bottom out," have a car crash or develop some serious health problem before you address your concerns. Do something now. Remember, addiction is treatable. And there are sensitive, trained healthcare providers who can help you decide how to proceed.

In any intervention – informal or formal – it's important to approach your loved one when he or she is not high or drunk – and when you're not deeply upset.

Here are some additional tips:

- Stay calm
- Couch your comments in concern
- Avoid labeling the person an "alcoholic" or "addict."
- Cite specific incidents resulting from the person's substance abuse (you were recently arrested for DWI.")
- Stick to what you know firsthand, not hearsay
- Talk in "I statements," explaining how the person's behavior has affected you ("When you drive drunk, I don't sleep all night.")
- Be prepared for denial and resentment

- Be supportive and hopeful about change

What are the Necessary Steps for a Formal Intervention?

A formal or structured intervention is a group meeting designed to help the substance user understand the problem and the need to take action and seek treatment.

The first step in a formal intervention is to gather all the significant people in a substance user's life, such as immediate and extended family members, physicians, friends, employers, coworkers, religious advisors, neighbors – anyone who can describe the physical and emotional changes and damages they see and experience.

Next this group meets with a professional, such as a family therapist or substance use counselor, to learn how to express their concern in a constructive way. The professional educates them about what to expect during the intervention and afterwards, and how they can organize their comments to avoid blaming and to increase the chance that the person will hear their messages.

Then, the group of concerned individuals and their professional guide meet with the substance user for a conversation. They express caring and concern, presenting facts about the impact that the substance use has had on them. They convey that they are unwilling to continue to overlook the damage that substance use is having on the person in need and on many others. They press the person to admit that a substance use problem exists and that it is causing many other problems.

The goal of an intervention is to get the person to agree to get help (attend a treatment program) immediately. Just promising to stop is considered an unacceptable outcome. Participants must clearly spell out the consequences each will impose if the person refuses treatment. These types of ultimatums can have life-threatening implications, which is why including a professional guide is so important.

10 Tips for a Formal Intervention

Goal: to have the person begin treatment immediately.

1. Enlist a professional to help plan the intervention.

2. Bring together the people most significant to the user (3 to 6 is best, no children) – the people who are concerned and who have clout with him or her. Only include people who are comfortable with the process.

3. Have a plan – decide who is going to say what.

4. Make all arrangements for the person to begin treatment immediately following the intervention. Know the insurance details and which hospital or treatment facility.

5. Identify the objections you might hear from the substance user and be prepared to answer each one.

6. Decide what consequences you're prepared to follow through with if the person refuses to enter treatment. For a teenager, it might be: "We will file a petition with the court to have you placed in treatment." For a spouse: "I will no longer cover up for you," or even: "I won't remain in this relationship with you."

7. Be prepared to follow through with these consequences if treatment is refused.

8. Tell the person that you care about him or her but explain what you are concerned about. Bring a list of examples. Be truthful and clear. Example: We love you very much, but…

9. Rehearse the intervention at least once. Know your roles.

10. Get a commitment from the person that they're willing to get help and get them there immediately.

Mandating Treatment

The vast majority of people who enter substance abuse treatment do so because of external pressure. Research has shown that required, or mandated, treatment is an effective motivator. Keep in mind that involuntary treatment can work just as well as voluntary treatment.

Why would people change if they are being forced? Wouldn't they change faster if they sought treatment voluntarily? Perhaps. But by mandating treatment, people are left with a choice: enter treatment, or lose something important to them: For example:

- Individuals arrested for driving while intoxicated may be ordered by the court to attend a driver education program and receive weekly counseling to avoid jail and keep their driver's license.
- Mothers whose ability to care for their children is compro-

mised due to substance use disorders may be required to attend treatment so their children are not placed in foster care.

- Employees found using substances on the job may be required to attend substance abuse treatment or lose their job.

The threat of losing important relationships, good health, or reputation may motivate some to enter treatment, even if they are not enthusiastic about doing so. For this reason, the person in need should clearly hear that friends and family members will lose trust, respect, and even regular contact if the substance use continues.

What About Requiring Abstinence?

Some families tell the person to stop all drinking and drug use. However, complying can be difficult – uncontrollable alcohol or other drug craving, seeking, and use is the hallmark of addiction. If you decide to give an ultimatum, require treatment, not abstinence. People who engage in treatment will be better able to achieve abstinence, because they will be given the medical attention and emotional support they need to maintain abstinence over the long term.

What About People Who Recover Without Going to Treatment?

While treatment is not absolutely necessary for recovery, a person's ability to recover without treatment varies widely. Some people use prayer, self-help groups, active church participation, the power of example, or a very supportive employer or group of friends to recover. Others don't have the same network or life philosophy. A health care professional or substance use counselor will be able to help you make treatment decisions.

What If My Loved One Relapses?

Since addiction is a chronic disease, relapses do occur. If this happens, don't lose hope. A relapse doesn't mean that the person isn't trying, or that his/her recovery is "failing." The majority of people with addictions who are in recovery suffer at least one relapse along the way.

If relapse occurs, get back in touch with the professional or self-help group that you've worked with in the past, and prepare to intervene again. But remember, ultimately you are not in control of whether your loved one stays in recovery. You can only control how you react to his or her behavior – and how you conduct your own life.

Intervention Resources

For more information about formal interventions, or to find someone who can help you, contact

>*The National Council on Alcoholism and Drug Dependence*
>*National Intervention Network*
>*1-800-622-2255 or*
>*www. ncadd.org/programs/nin/index.html or*
>
>*The Intervention Resource Center*
>*1-888-421-4321 or www. interventioninfo.org.*

For more on informal interventions, visit our Helping Others with a Problem section. (www.drugfree.org)

Find out more about Treatment and Recovery (www.drugfree.org)

(Sources: Mary Ann Amodeo, Ph.D, Join together, Herbert D. Kleber, MD, and "Moyers on Addiction: How to Approach an Intervention" by Donna Boundy, from the companion web site to the 5 part PBS series Moyers On Addiction: Close to Home. Used with permission).

Methadone

The ongoing controversy.
Is the Cure worse than the Disease?

FOR THE HIGH METHADONE USER WHO IS TRAPPED - THERE IS NOW HOPE

By Steve Hayes, Director Novus Detox Center New Port Richey, FL

Methadone, an opioid, was first produced in 1939 at the pharmaceutical laboratories of I.G. Farben in Germany. Named Amidon, and although there is evidence that some testing was done of the drug, there is no evidence that it was widely used by the Germans in World War II because they feared it was too addictive.

After the war, the German patents on Amidon and other drugs were voided and Amidon was tested and released in the United States by Eli Lilly in 1947 as Dolophine. Dolophine was derived from the Latin word dolor (pain) and finis (end).

Later Dolophine came to be known as methadone. Originally marketed as a pain reliever, it was not until the 1960's, when the number of heroin addicts was accelerating and the negative impact on society became widely known, did the idea of converting the heroin addict to a methadone addict become accepted as a treatment procedure.

ONE ADDICTION TRADED FOR ANOTHER

The advocates of substituting methadone for heroin were aware that methadone was often more addictive than heroin. However, heroin users were creating many problems for society. In order to purchase their heroin, they were committing crimes like robbery, prostitution and even murder. In addition, these heroin users were spreading sexually transmitted diseases and also HIV from their contaminated needles.

These heroin addicts were flooding emergency rooms due to overdoses, or because they got a bad batch of heroin, or because they contracted hepatitis. Having these addicts switch to a drug that they could take orally like cough syrup that was "legal" and much less expensive, was appealing to many in our society.

Heroin users are forced to obtain a "fix" every 4-6 hours or they will start experiencing painful withdrawals. (Withdrawal means that the body is craving the endorphins produced by the heroin and this leads to sickness. One of our patients who had experienced it said that it was ten times worse than the worst flu they ever had.)

This is one of the reasons why most heroin addicts don't even attempt to hold down "regular" jobs. Besides, few legitimate jobs provide sufficient income to allow them to pay for their habit.

No one could argue that heroin addiction was a terrible thing, and getting people off heroin sounded good if you forgot or ignored the other facts about methadone---it creates many of the same effects as heroin and is even more addictive than heroin. In a classic example of "the end justifies the means", the FDA was persuaded that even though heroin was illegal, it was ok for methadone, a drug that is more addictive and creates many of the same effects, to be legal.

 Instead of rewarding criminals who smuggled heroin into the country for sale so people could be addicted, the FDA chose to reward drug manufacturers and people who run methadone clinics so that the same people could continue to be addicted.

There is a heated political debate over whether we should legalize drugs and take the profits away from the criminals. We cut out the illegal dealers and gave the profits to drug companies and to methadone clinics-which are limited in number and thus assuring their profitability.

THE PROMISE
In summary, switching heroin users to methadone seemed to provide

a solution to society's problems.

Methadone has a much longer half life than heroin (half-life is the amount of time before half of a drug taken is excreted from the body), so a person can normally be given one dose of methadone and this would last until the next day.

Methadone doesn't cost $300 a day but only $300 a month and often this can be paid by a government program.

· Heroin addicts no longer have to participate in illegal activities to obtain their drugs.

· Heroin addicts are no longer using needles to inject heroin and this will reduce the spread of many diseases.

· People in society no longer have to feel guilty about not addressing the heroin addiction problem because the methadone advocates promoted the use of methadone as a step toward helping the addict stop taking drugs of any kind.

THE FACTS

However, what was promised about methadone was not delivered. We now know these facts about methadone:

A 1999 study done at the University of London found that methadone actually increased the cravings for heroin. Many methadone users supplement their "high" with other illegal drugs like prescription narcotics or even heroin. (Illegal drug dealers now can be found around these clinics because business is brisk).

· Most methadone users are forced to come to the methadone clinics and wait in long lines every day or at least once a week. Because the number of methadone clinics is limited by law, some methadone users have to drive 50-80 miles a day and when they arrive, stand in line for an hour or more to get their methadone dose that will keep them from going into withdrawal, and then they go to work.

· The first thing a methadone addict often must do when considering moving is not check on the schools for their children but on the location of the nearest methadone clinic.

· Almost all of the people who switched to methadone from heroin have seen the amount of their daily methadone dose increase-to 100 milligrams or even much higher. In most cases the addict is now taking a much higher dosage of methadone than the equivalent amount of heroin that they were using.

· Almost none of these former heroin addicts have been able to wean themselves off methadone. (Some complain that the methadone clinics don't help their clients wean off. Apparently many clinics tell the methadone addict who is trying to taper down but experiences some withdrawal symptoms that if they are experiencing any discomfort, then the dose should be increased back to where it was. Some clinics apparently tell people that "They are addicts and will always have to take methadone." But this is not too surprising-the methadone clinics only stay in business if their clients remain addicted.)

· Even if the methadone addict who is now taking 80 to 240 milligrams of methadone decides that he or she has to stop, there are few rehabilitation centers that will accept people on more than 80 milligrams per day, so the person has to either face serious withdrawal pains, find one of the few medical detox centers that will accept high dosage methadone users, or stay on methadone.

· The real truth is that switching an addict to a different addiction never really made sense. The real solution was and will always be to help the addict become drug-free.

THE TRAP
No responsible person can dispute the fact that as the doses of opioids like methadone or oxycodone increase, people's cognitive abilities and their reaction time are adversely affected more and more. They can also experience other side effects such as being more susceptible to illnesses.

Perhaps the saddest part of the methadone experiment is that our society encourages these former heroin addicts to take more and more methadone, since it costs the same if the dose is 10 milligrams or 200 milligrams.

Every time a methadone addict gets clean, the only groups that lose are the drug companies that produce methadone and the methadone clinics who lose money. The rest of society wins and the former methadone addict wins most of all.

THE SOLUTION--REHAB
There are many effective rehabilitation facilities that are successful in helping people become drug-free. These rehabilitation facilities are

located all over the world.

However, despite the desire of these rehabilitation facilities to help, few if any will accept someone on a dose of methadone over 80 milligrams per day. The methadone addict that calls is told that they must first bring their methadone usage down to 20-40 milligrams per day and the rehabilitation facility will gladly accept them.

The truth is that most methadone addicts who seek help have tried to withdraw or at least cut down their dose of methadone in the past. Almost all of these people were unsuccessful because they began experiencing painful withdrawal symptoms and stopped their taper.

Unfortunately, many of them ended up taking more methadone than they were taking when they started trying to withdraw, and their despair of ever being free of the monster called methadone grew.

The rehabilitation facilities who are not able to accept these methadone addicts have tried to refer them to medical detox facilities, but they have found that there are very few medical detox facilities that will accept a methadone patient taking over 80 milligrams a day of methadone. Some facilities that do accept the patients simply put them in a room and give them some drugs that help alleviate some of the pain, but the patient has some very difficult withdrawal symptoms and often leaves the detox center before completing their withdrawal. Then they go back to the methadone clinic and the despair grows even more.

The solution is to locate a medical detox center that will assist a person on an 80 milligram or higher daily dose of methadone complete their withdrawal more comfortably, safely and more quickly from the drug.

"A junkie is someone who uses their body to tell society that something is wrong."

Stella Adler, actress, acting coach

Methadone Changed My Life

By Nancy Garvin
Mother, Nurse, Advocate.

I had heard of Methadone but only in a vague sense as its use for heroin addiction. I had no idea how this drug would soon change my life forever. I was not up to date on the current uses that had swept the medical profession in the last few years. If only I had known maybe everything would have turned out differently.

My son, Robby, had been diagnosed with some back problems that led him from an Orthopedic doctor to a pain management specialist. I thought it was somewhat odd for Robby to be referred to pain management as he did not suffer extensive pain every day. Although one doctor recommended surgery another had said, "Definitely not, you are only twenty four years old." There was a 50/50 chance there could be permanent effects from such a surgery and that was enough for Robby to fear such an operation at this time. He then went to his first visit to address his discomfort in March 2006. He was then scheduled to visit this doctor once every month.

June 2008, Robby arrived for his fourth visit to this pain expert. Previous visits resulted in prescriptions of drugs that bothered Robby in some form or another. Robby had no history of prescription or illicit drug abuse. He was particular about his medical care and kept close accounts of any treatments. On this Friday afternoon Robby called me from the doctor's office and asked me, "Momma, what is methadone?"

I asked him why did he want to know and he explained that the doctor had written him a prescription for it. I had concern as to why this doctor would give a drug that was used for hard core heroin addicts to my son. So, I suggested that Robby call our pharmacy with any questions. I then had learned that they were using it for pain and never gave it a second thought to any possible dangers that may lie ahead from its use.

Robby and his friend Joey had already made plans to go out of town for the weekend, leaving that Friday evening. He left his doctor's office, filled his new prescriptions, and then traveled to a nearby town to pick up Joey. Since Robby had no idea how this drug would make him feel, he waited until later that evening when he had reached his destination and was settled in the hotel room for the night.

It was there when he took his first dose of methadone. He even sat and wrote out a timed schedule for dosing as according to the bottle's directions. It read that he could take 1-2, 10 mg tablets every eight hours. Initially he took one pill to test the effects of this unknown drug. The following morning he took another dose of one pill then proceeded for their day at a local theme park. After a full day of walking Robby took two Methadone pills as his back was causing him more pain then normal. Since he had already taken two doses of a single pill he felt he could handle increasing the dosage as it was directed to take two if needed, again following the hourly schedule.

Robby still lived at home but when he was away, even for just a short period it was not uncommon for him to call me, even for the littlest topic. That Saturday evening he called several times with the last call ending about 2:30 AM. The last words I heard from his voice was, "I love you Mom." The following morning after he woke up he told Joey he was not up to another day at the park and felt like he had over-done it the day before. He took his 10:00 AM dose and lay back down to rest. By 2:00 PM that afternoon he had taken his last breath while sleeping.

I had received one call from Joey telling me they were transporting Robby to the hospital by ambulance but all he could say was, "Mom, I have never seen him like this." Joey knew how serious Robby's condition was but did not have the heart to tell me. About forty-five minutes went by then the phone rang again. As I answered the call a women's voice was on the other end. She said, "Ms. Garvin," I replied, "yes." "It is my understanding that you were aware your son was being brought to the emergency room." Again I said, "Yes."

She followed with, "I am sorry to inform you, we did what we could, but your son did not make it." At that moment my world as I had known it ended, never to be the same. Sometime later Joey called from the hospital. I could barely speak as I was mentally distraught.

He told me he was with Robby as we talked and I begged him to make sure he was not breathing, maybe they made a mistake. Maybe it was not my son they were talking about. But, it was true as Joey confided. "Momma, he is not breathing, he is gone." I asked him to hold him for me, kiss him and tell him how much I love him.

Of course it was some time before we were notified of the true cause of his untimely death, but I knew in my heart shortly afterwards. Call it a mother's intuition, a gut feeling or whatever but I knew it was the Methadone that killed my son. The initial autopsy did not show a definite cause so we had to wait weeks for the toxicology report to come in. Finally, cause of death was METHADONE TOXICITY.

June 11th, 2008 will mark two years since that day that would change my life forever. There is not a day that goes by that I do not think of or cry for my son. I miss him so very much. In the beginning I truly did not think I was going to make it through my grief and even had concerns that mentally I was not strong enough. Over the years I have lost loved ones, my father, grand parents and so many close friends but nothing compares to the loss of a child. I have even thought at times that had he died from cancer or an auto accident that it would give me a better understanding of how a fairly healthy, 24-year-old, loving young man could die. The need to seek and find the answers started shortly after his passing.

Long before we received the confirmed report of Robby's death I started my venture of research with an endless path to investigate. At first I only looked at the drug itself and the association of its use for pain management. I immediately filed a non-profit organization status with the IRS and named it Mothers Against Medical Abuse.Org, nicknamed MAMA.Org. As a nurse and in the medical field for twenty years, losing Robby to a lethal drug and a doctor's negligence, I had enough. Early in my research of methadone I reached out to the people behind its manufacturing and distribution; my findings were alarming. They truly had no clue or just did not care that this drug was killing so many innocent lives.

Two years ago little was being said by the media about Methadone and the trail of devastation it was leaving in its path. Actually, Methadone has been killing people for some time but they were mostly IV heroin drug users and their death was associated to "just another overdose related death." As Methadone increased in popularity for distribution so have the death tolls.

Currently, methadone is the leading cause of death by a single prescription narcotic. More people are dying from methadone than the heroin it was used to treat. After talking to dozens of families in the beginning of my research I questioned the validity of safety that is given with this drug. I immediately knew this drug was much more lethal than they warn. There were too many variations of victims and the only common bond was Methadone. This triggered a need to investigate further and we launched an autopsy research project in late 2007.

Donated reports come from the families of the victims themselves. These deaths have a direct link to clinical use, pain management or the diversion from both sources. You do not have to abuse this drug to die as many were under the care and monitoring of a doctor during their demise. The risks are greater when another substance is mixed with Methadone, but Methadone is very deadly all by itself and in very small doses. A recent study has validated what I have been saying for almost two years, ***"Methadone is lethal in therapeutic doses."*** So why is nothing being done to help protect the consumer who is unaware of the possible dangers?

For years Methadone has been used for substitution of an addict's drug of choice and this has become a socially acceptable practice. Pro-Methadone Advocates which include representatives from drug companies, healthcare groups, operating clinics and the users themselves have assisted in the misconception of this drug.

A common slogan used is, "Methadone saves lives." This phrase has led to a false sense of safety among a large portion of this country. Clinics using Methadone make many claims that appear to be impressive and greatly needed in our current culture. After months of investigating these practices and even spending time with the addicts themselves I found much of this praise to be over dramatized and seldom factual.

In most cases these clinics are not detoxifying their patrons as they claim but keep them on a highly addictive narcotic for years, many for a lifetime. Opening methadone clinics has become a gold mine with an enormous potential for profits. It is not in the best interest to produce drug free patrons so excuses are made as to why these people must stay on drug replacement as the best means for treating addiction.

This practice brings satisfaction to many. The addict supplements his addictive cravings, clinical investors are making millions, and families do see a difference in their loved one. Is the addict still an active addict while on methadone? Yes, and if they do not receive their daily dose they will experience withdrawals that are often described to be extremely more intense than coming off of heroin. Due to the long half life of methadone and how it stores in the body, withdrawals can last for weeks instead of days versus other opiates. The stories from former methadone users differ greatly than the current proclamations. With drug abuse in its current epidemic, is providing legalized drug substitution stations the answer to addiction? Some will swear by it and others will die by it as methadone ravages this nation.

The knowledge I have gained in almost two years has opened many doors in the Methadone saga and brought about questions as to why such a lethal drug could gain so much respect. Recently the media and family members of victims have been reaching out for answers. Telling their stories of heartache and loss has become their only outlet for an inner peace that may never be reached. Even our own Federal agencies ignore these cries for help as the death tolls rise. So maybe some of us carry a different definition of "saving lives."

Some thought they had finally found the hope they were looking for only to lose their loved one only days after entering a clinical facility; cause of death, methadone toxicity. With an over-abundance of prescribing, Methadone is on every street corner and those just looking for a one night high take one pill and could die.

There is nothing else like this drug on the market today and no hope of regulations to control this problem. Methadone will most likely go down in medical history as the most controversial drug marketed in our era. One side swears it to be the "wonder drug" and others damn its existence. Thousands continue to die who were never told of the dangers that lurked in their potential darkness.

For me "saving lives" means to never let another parent feel my pain, to let everyone know how lethal this drug is and hope they will choose a safer alternative, to allow the public to make a knowledge-able choice if they want to take the risk of consuming this product.

This was never an offer to my son who had no idea he was ingesting a death sentence. We as human beings and consumers have the right to know if a product or treatment may cause death and properly in-form the person prior to prescribing. Not with Methadone. They never tell the potential victim that thousands have died. Instead they preach their formatted praise.

No one is safe from becoming Methadone's next victim. Methadone is a legal drug but if you try it you must be willing to die for it.

Nancy Garvin is the author of the book – "40 Hours To Die, A Methadone Story." Please log on to her website listed below for the publication date.

(www. mothersagainstmedicalabuse.org)

THE TEEN BRAIN

Being a parent is undoubtedly one of the hardest jobs you will ever have, and love. My husband and I often wonder how many people there would be on the planet if every man and woman knew the nature and scope of parenting, the tremendous highs but sometimes the horrible lows, before undertaking this awesome, life-changing responsibility.

Our children are our delight, our joy. We would do anything for them. They coo and giggle when little babies and make us swell with pride. We dote on their first steps, their first words, all their firsts. We marvel that our hearts can hold so much love for them without bursting.

And yet...one day that darling love of your life, that little angel, seems to don devil's horns and does what he/she can to drive you crazy. You wonder what happened to that bundle of sweetness who you cradled in your arms so lovingly, the little ones who loved you to read to them and tuck them into bed with kisses and hugs, who would cling to you, and be happy to be with you.

Then one day they're approaching the teen years, the tweens, and nothing is ever the same. Suddenly you, the parent don't know anything. You are someone to be argued with, someone they might ask to drop them off a block from their friend's home so they wouldn't have to be seen with you, someone who disciplines them just to be mean, and someone with whom they don't want to spend too much time.

Not every family will go through this of course, and not every family will experience more than a little of the above named behavior but one thing's for sure; the teen years will bring more than their fair share of ups and downs for all concerned.

A funny line comes to mind (I paraphrase here); a comedian said that some anthropologists claim that teenagers aren't even remotely related to us! It sounds funny but how many of us don't think there might be a kernel of truth to that? Teenagers are definitely different! And as much as we love them, wholeheartedly and unconditionally, sometimes we just don't understand them...even though we were once teens ourselves.

Here then is A Parent's Guide to the Teen Brain excerpted from A Parent's Guide to the Teen Brain by the Partnership For a Drug-Free America. We're certain this will help you understand that adorable/ maddening, lovely/moody, emotional/detached, agreeable/ argumentative, kind/selfish being known as a Teen.

Please note this is not a comprehensive report of the Teen Brain. For complete information including tests you can take, videos you can watch and more, and for complete understanding of the science behind A Parent's Guide to the Teen Brain please go to www .drugfree.org/teenbrain/science/index.html

Is My Teen's Attitude and Behavior Normal?

From mood swings to risk taking, "normal teenage behavior" can appear to be anything-but-normal to parents and other bystanders. However, new research reveals that patterns of brain development during these formative years play a significant role in shaping your teen's personality and actions.

New discoveries about adolescent brain development have opened up fresh ways of thinking about teen behavior, and offer new insight into how parents can help their teens understand the risks of drugs and alcohol. For instance:

Scientific evidence reveals that the brain is fully mature at about age 25 — much later than previously believed.

One of the last areas of the brain to develop is the Prefrontal Cortex, which is responsible for processing information, making judgments, controlling impulses, and foreseeing consequences.

This new information throws into stark relief the major risks of teenage substance use, including the possibility of causing permanent neurological damage to the developing brain. Concerned parents want to know how to apply these findings to real life. That's what **A Parent's Guide to the Teen Brain** is all about.

Through an entertaining and compelling mix of media — video, interactive segments, scenario-based role-playing experiences, expert advice, and practical tips — **A Parent's Guide to the Teen Brain** illustrates the links between teen behavior and the big changes happening in teen brains. In doing so, the site offers parents the keys to keeping their own perspective while guiding their teens more effectively through this tumultuous time of life.

The Partnership for a Drug-Free America partnered with Treatment Research Institute and WGBH Educational Foundation to develop **A Parent's Guide to the Teen Brain**.

Scientists are beginning to learn that it takes a brain about 25 years to fully develop, and that a huge burst of development happens during adolescence. That burst can explain a lot of unpredictable – and sometimes risky – teen behavior.

● Adolescent brain development

Scientists now know that the brain is getting reorganized in a big way during the teenage years. This is a time of huge opportunities — and risks.

Everyone knows the importance of guiding and nurturing toddlers, whose brains are developing at warp speed. But what about the development of the teen brain? We're now learning that adolescents go through a similar wave of major development. From ages 13 to about age 25, a **pruning and strengthening process** is happening in their brains. During that time, the brain cells and neural connections that get used the least get pruned away and die off; those that get used the most get stronger.

This new knowledge about adolescent brain development explains why it's so important for parents to encourage teens to have healthy activities: The more time your teen spends learning music, the stronger those brain connections get. The same is true of the connections she uses for playing video games, mastering a sport, or watching TV.

Ironically, this period — when the brain is rapidly changing and most vulnerable to outside influences — is when teens are most likely to experiment with drugs and alcohol. Why? One reason may be because the brain region that's responsible for making complex judgments (the prefrontal cortex) isn't fully mature, and therefore is prone to being overpowered by the emotional or motivational regions that are more mature. Scientists believe this aspect of teenage brain development explains why young people sometimes use poor judgment and don't have good impulse control.

Because of the huge changes happening in the teenage brain, it's possible that a decision your teen makes now may affect him for life. (Brain scans, for instance, have linked alcohol abuse with decreased memory functioning.[1]) Just sharing that fact with your teen may help him to stop and think before he takes any chances, and even inspire him to make more healthy choices.

● Adolescent brain and behavior

From early adolescence through their mid-20s, a teen's brain develops somewhat unevenly, from back to front. This may help explain their endearingly quirky behavior but also makes them prone to risk-taking.

The parts of the adolescent brain which develop first are those which control physical coordination, emotion and motivation. However, the part of the brain which controls reasoning and impulses - known as the Prefrontal Cortex - is near the front of the brain and, therefore, develops last. This part of the brain does not fully mature until the age of 25.

It's as if, while the other parts of the teen brain are shouting, the Prefrontal Cortex is not quite ready to play referee. This can have noticeable effects on adolescent behavior. You may have noticed some of these effects in your teen:

- difficulty holding back or controlling emotions,
- a preference for physical activity,
- a preference for high excitement and low effort activities (video games, sex, drugs, rock 'n' roll),
- poor planning and judgement (rarely thinking of negative consequences),
- more risky, impulsive behaviors, including experimenting with drugs and alcohol.

The development of the adolescent brain and behavior are closely linked. In a wink, hormones can shift your teen's emotions into overdrive, leading to unpredictable - and sometimes risky - actions. Unfortunately, developing brains may be more prone to damage. This means that experimentation with drugs and alcohol can have lasting, harmful effects on your teen's health.

- Research shows that alcohol abuse during the teenage years negatively impacts the memory center of the brain (the hippocampus).
- The use of drugs and alcohol may also disrupt the development of the adolescent brain in unhealthy ways, making it harder for teens to cope with social situations and the normal pressures of life.
- Moreover, the brain's reward circuits (the dopamine system) get thrown out of whack when under the influence. This causes a teen to feel in a funk when not using drugs or alcohol - and going back for more only makes things worse.

It is important to urge your teen to take healthy risks. Not only will participation in constructive activities - such as athletics or the arts - help him or her form positive lifestyle habits, it will help your teen's forebrain develop as well.

● Effects of drugs on the brain & teen moods

Finding ways to satisfy needs and desires is part of life. It's one of the many skills that is being fine-tuned during the teen years. When a teen takes drugs, it can interfere with his natural ability to feel good. Here's how drugs affect the brain:

The brain is made up of billions of nerve cells. Nerves control everything from when his heart beats to what he feels, thinks and does. They do this by sending electrical signals throughout his body. The signals get passed from nerve, to nerve by chemical messengers called "neurotransmitters."

For example, some of the signals that neurotransmitters send cause a feeling of satisfaction or pleasure. These natural rewards are the body's way of making sure we look for more of what makes us feel good. (For instance, when we eat something tasty, neurotransmitters tell us we feel good. Seeking more of this pleasure helps to ensure we don't starve.) The main neurotransmitter of the "feel-good" message is called dopamine.

All drugs of abuse overload the body with dopamine — in other words, they cause the reward system to send too many "feel-good" signals. In response, the body's brain systems try to right the balance by letting fewer of the "feel-good" signals through. As time goes on, the body needs more of the drug to feel the same high as before. This effect is known as "tolerance."

The effects of drugs on the brain don't just end when the high wears off. When a person stops taking a drug, his dopamine levels are low for some time. He may feel down, or flat, and unable to feel the normal pleasures in life, even when meeting a basic life need. His brain will eventually restore the dopamine balance by itself, but it takes time — anywhere from hours, to days, or even months, depending on the drug, the length and amount of abuse, and the person.

Because they have an overactive impulse to seek pleasure and less ability to consider the consequences, teens are especially vulnerable when it comes to the temptations of drugs and alcohol. And because the internal reward systems are still being developed, a teen's ability to bounce back to normal after abusing drugs may be compromised due to how drugs affect the brain.

What Can You Do?

- Help Teens while their brains develop
- Encourage risk-taking and giving back
- Pick your battles
- Talk about drugs and alcohol

Note: The above section "What Can You Do?" is covered completely in the online site - A Parent's Guide to the Teen Brain.

Typical Teen Behaviors – Do Any of these sound familiar?

- **Impulsive**
- **Rebellious**
- **Style-obsessed**
- **Irritable**
- **Noncommunicative**
- **Friend-Centered**
- **Risk Taker**
- **Sleep Deprived**

Impulsive— Consequences always come as a surprise to this teen. Think it through? I don't think so. She'll buy a $300 final-sale dress, on your credit card and then ask if it's okay when the bill comes. Responsibility? You'll have to work with her on that one.

Rebellious — She's not bad but there she is pushing back mightily against even the smallest of boundaries. She tests limits, breaks rules and plays "Devil's Advocate" like a natural. You love her…but sometimes you don't like her so much.

Style-Obsessed — This teen's a walking billboard. His clothes, his accessories, his gadgets: everything has got to have this week's version of the right label. And don't even get him started on your (ahem) taste.

Irritable — This teen can go from irritable to laughing in the blink of an eye. For you, it's exhausting trying to keep up, never knowing which kid you're going to get. And it seems you are always to blame. Wait! Never mind. That was a smile!

Noncommunicative — "How was your day?" "Great." "What do you want for dinner?" "Whatever." Perfect! If she spoke any less, she could be a mime. But then again, she talks with her friends all the time. You know this; you get the phone bill.

Friend-centered — Your teen's new slogan: "I am IM." That little device against his ear, that's his entire circle of friends, coming with you wherever you go. When did friends become as important – MORE important even – than family?

Risk-Taker — This teen likes the adrenaline rush of EXTREME sports, EXTREME experimentation, and, apparently, EXTREME not-listening-to-your-advice. Whatever he does he makes it exciting (for him) and terrifying (for you).

Sleep-deprived — This teen is overscheduled, overwired and over-due for a good night's rest. She stays up too late, then sleeps until noon. It's as if she just flew in from halfway across the world, and is still living in a different time zone.

Well friends, I hope you found the above "A Parent's Guide to the Teen Brain" as informative, interesting, and fascinating as my husband and I have. Our regret is that this information was not widely available or known to most parents, and certainly not to us, while our own son was struggling with addiction and we were struggling with his teen years. We hope the above will help you in dealing with your teen and we're very thankful to the Partnership For a Drug-Free America for allowing us to reprint their information here.

Again, to read A Parent's Guide to the Teen Brain in its entirety, please visit:

(http://www.drugfree.org/teenbrain/index.html)

"Statistics prove that teenage Internet gambling is the fastest growing addiction of the day, akin to drug and alcohol abuse in the 1930s, ... It's pernicious, it's evil, it's certainly one that feeds on those who are the weakest members of society -- and that's the young and the poor."

David Robertson

An excerpt from NIDA

(National Institute On Drug Abuse)

September, 2007

"Many people do not understand why individuals become addicted to drugs or how drugs change the brain to foster compulsive drug abuse. They mistakenly view drug abuse and addiction as strictly a social problem and may characterize those who take drugs as morally weak. One very common belief is that drug abusers should be able to just stop taking drugs if they are only willing to change their behavior. What people often underestimate is the complexity of drug addiction—that it is a disease that impacts the brain and because of that, stopping drug abuse is not simply a matter of willpower. Through scientific advances we now know much more about how exactly drugs work in the brain, and we also know that drug addiction can be successfully treated to help people stop abusing drugs and resume their productive lives.

What is drug addiction?

Addiction is a chronic, often relapsing brain disease that causes compulsive drug seeking and use despite harmful consequences to the individual that is addicted and to those around them.

Drug addiction is a brain disease because the abuse of drugs leads to changes in the structure and function of the brain. Although it is true that for most people the initial decision to take drugs is voluntary, over time the changes in the brain caused by repeated drug abuse can affect a person's self control and ability to make sound decisions, and at the same time send intense impulses to take drugs.

It is because of these changes in the brain that it is so challenging for a person who is addicted to stop abusing drugs. Fortunately, there are treatments that help people to counteract addiction's powerful disruptive effects and regain control. Research shows that combining addiction treatment medications, if available, with behavioral therapy is the best way to ensure success for most patients. Treatment approaches that are tailored to each patient's drug abuse patterns and any co-occurring medical, psychiatric, and social problems can lead to sustained recovery and a life without drug abuse.

Similar to other chronic, relapsing diseases, such as diabetes, asthma, or heart disease, drug addiction can be managed successfully. And, as with other chronic diseases, it is not uncommon for a person to relapse and begin abusing drugs again. Relapse, however, does not signal failure—rather, it indicates that treatment should be reinstated, adjusted, or that alternate treatment is needed to help the individual regain control and recover.

What happens to your brain when you take drugs?

Drugs are chemicals that tap into the brain's communication system and disrupt the way nerve cells normally send, receive, and process information. There are at least two ways that drugs are able to do this: (1) by imitating the brain's natural chemical messengers, and/or (2) by over stimulating the "reward circuit" of the brain.

Some drugs, such as marijuana and heroin, have a similar structure to chemical messengers, called neurotransmitters, which are naturally produced by the brain. Because of this similarity, these drugs are able to "fool" the brain's receptors and activate nerve cells to send abnormal messages.

Other drugs, such as cocaine or methamphetamine, can cause the nerve cells to release abnormally large amounts of natural neurotransmitters, or prevent the normal recycling of these brain chemicals, which is needed to shut off the signal between neurons. This disruption produces a greatly amplified message that ultimately disrupts normal communication patterns.

Nearly all drugs, directly or indirectly, target the brain's reward system by flooding the circuit with dopamine. Dopamine is a neurotransmitter present in regions of the brain that control movement, emotion, motivation, and feelings of pleasure. The over stimulation of this system, which normally responds to natural behaviors that are linked to survival eating, spending time with loved ones, (etc.), produces euphoric effects in response to the drugs. This reaction sets in motion a pattern that "teaches" people to repeat the behavior of abusing drugs.

As a person continues to abuse drugs, the brain adapts to the overwhelming surges in dopamine by producing less dopamine or by reducing the number of dopamine receptors in the reward circuit. As a result, dopamine's impact on the reward circuit is lessened, reducing the abuser's ability to enjoy the drugs and the things that previously brought pleasure. This decrease compels those addicted to drugs to keep abusing drugs in order to attempt to bring their dopamine function back to normal. And, they may now require larger amounts of the drug than they first did to achieve the dopamine high—an effect known as tolerance.

Long-term abuse causes changes in other brain chemical systems and circuits as well. Glutamate is a neurotransmitter that influences the reward circuit and the ability to learn. When the optimal concentration of glutamate is altered by drug abuse, the brain attempts to compensate, which can impair cognitive function. Drugs of abuse facilitate non-conscious (conditioned) learning, which leads the user to experience uncontrollable cravings when they see a place or person they associate with the drug experience, even when the drug itself is not available.

Brain imaging studies of drug-addicted individuals show changes in areas of the brain that are critical to judgment, decision making, learning and memory, and behavior control. Together, these changes can drive an abuser to seek out and take drugs compulsively despite adverse consequences— in other words, to become addicted to drugs.

Why do some people become addicted and others do not?

No single factor can predict whether or not a person will become addicted to drugs. Risk for addiction is influenced by a person's biology, social environment, and age or stage of development. The more risk factors an individual has, the greater the chance that taking drugs can lead to addiction. For example:

Biology. The genes that people are born with—in combination with environmental influences—account for about half of their addiction vulnerability. Additionally, gender, ethnicity, and the presence of other mental disorders may influence risk for drug abuse and addiction.

Environment. A person's environment includes many different influences— from family and friends to socioeconomic status and quality of life in general. Factors such as peer pressure, physical and sexual abuse, stress, and parental involvement can greatly influence the course of drug abuse and addiction in a person's life.

Development. Genetic and environmental factors interact with critical developmental stages in a person's life to affect addiction vulnerability, and adolescents experience a double challenge.

Although taking drugs at any age can lead to addiction, the earlier that drug use begins, the more likely it is to progress to more serious abuse. And because adolescents' brains are still developing in the areas that govern decision making, judgment, and self-control, they are especially prone to risk-taking behaviors, including trying drugs of abuse.

Prevention is the key

Drug addiction is a preventable disease. Results from NIDA-funded research have shown that prevention programs that involve families, schools, communities, and the media are effective in reducing drug abuse. Although many events and cultural factors affect drug abuse trends, when youths perceive drug abuse as harmful, they reduce their drug taking.

It is necessary, therefore, to help youth and the general public to understand the risks of drug abuse, and for teachers, parents, and healthcare professionals to keep sending the message that drug addiction can be prevented if a person never abuses drugs.

"Exploring Myths about Drug Abuse"

by **Alan I. Leshner, Ph.D.**, *Director,*

National Institute on Drug Abuse, National Institutes of Health

- **Myth: Drug addiction is voluntary behavior.**

A person starts out as an occasional drug user, and that is a voluntary decision. But as times passes, something happens, and that person goes from being a voluntary drug user to being a compulsive drug user. Why? Because over time, continued use of addictive drugs changes your brain -- at times in dramatic, toxic ways, at others in more subtle ways, but virtually always in ways that result in compulsive and even uncontrollable drug use.

- **Myth: More than anything else, drug addiction is a character flaw.**

Drug addiction is a brain disease. Every type of drug of abuse has its own individual mechanism for changing how the brain functions. But regardless of which drug a person is addicted to, many of the effects it has on the brain are similar: they range from changes in the molecules and cells that make up the brain, to mood changes, to changes in memory processes and in such motor skills as walking and talking. And these changes have a huge influence on all aspects of a person's behavior. The drug becomes the single most powerful motivator in a drug abuser's existence. He or she will do almost anything for the drug. This comes about because drug use has changed the individual's brain and its functioning in critical ways.

- **Myth: You have to want drug treatment for it to be effective.**

Virtually no one wants drug treatment. Two of the primary reasons people seek drug treatment are because the court ordered them to do so, or because loved ones urged them to seek treatment. Many scientific studies have shown convincingly that those who enter drug treatment programs in which they face "high pressure" to confront and attempt to surmount their addiction do comparatively better in treatment, regardless of the reason they sought treatment in the first place.

- **Myth: Treatment for drug addiction should be a one-shot deal.**

Like many other illnesses, drug addiction typically is a chronic disorder. To be sure, some people can quit drug use "cold turkey," or they can quit after receiving treatment just one time at a rehabilitation facility. But most of those who abuse drugs require longer-term treatment and, in many instances, repeated treatments.

- **Myth: We should strive to find a "magic bullet" to treat all forms of drug abuse.**

There is no "one size fits all" form of drug treatment, much less a magic bullet that suddenly will cure addiction. Different people have different drug abuse-related problems. And they respond very differently to similar forms of treatment, even when they're abusing the same drug. As a result, drug addicts need an array of treatments and services tailored to address their unique needs.

"Failure will never overtake me if my determination to succeed is strong enough."

Og Mandino, sales guru, author

Dear Parents,

I found the following article extremely informative about methamphetamine…and also very scary. After reading this, and other accounts of the dangers of methamphetamine use, I wanted to include this in the book.

When our children have gotten past the point of our brushing their teeth for them, and for keeping an eye on them to make sure they are diligent in their dental hygiene, we might overlook the impending signs of tooth decay. This article can serve as a reminder to keep an eye on them, making sure routine dental problems are just that… routine, and not the more insidious ravages of crystal meth use.

'Meth Mouth' can leave users toothless

Methamphetamine is a powerfully addictive drug that can seriously damage oral health, destroying a person's smile and natural ability to chew, according to the American Dental Association (ADA).

More than 12-million Americans have tried methamphetamine (also known as meth, crank, crystal and speed), which can be swallowed, injected, snorted or smoked, according to the 2004 National Survey on Drug Use and Health. The majority of users range between 18 and 34 years of age.

"Meth" users can go from having healthy teeth to extremely sensitive teeth and eventual tooth loss in about a year, warns the ADA. This condition is often called "meth mouth."

"Meth mouth robs people, especially young people of their teeth and frequently leads to full-mouth extractions and a lifetime of wearing dentures," says Robert M. Brandjord, ADA president. "Meth mouth is characterized by rampant tooth decay and teeth described by meth users as blackened, stained, rotting, crumbling or falling apart."

Dr. Brandjord explains, "The extensive tooth decay of meth mouth is attributed to the drug's dry-mouth effect and its propensity to cause cravings for high-calorie carbonated beverages, tooth grinding and clenching, and extended periods of poor oral hygiene."

"Very few people understand the broad dangers methamphetamine poses to the public health of our communities in addition to meth users themselves," says Stephen Pasierb, president and CEO, The Partnership for a Drug-Free America. "The ADA's warning should serve as a wake-up call to those who use this insidious drug as well as family and friends who are witness to this behavior, but not powerless to intervene and get the user the help they need. There is no safe level of meth use, but treatment and recovery are possible."

(Excerpted from www sciencedaily.com)

"The National Highway Traffic Safety Administration (NHTSA) reports that more than 17,000 people were killed in alcohol-related crashes in 2006.1 Studies also have found that drugs are used by 10 to 22 percent of drivers involved in crashes, often in combination with alcohol."

NIDA (NATIONAL INSTITUTE ON DRUG ABUSE)

Amphetamine abuse tied to heart attack at young age

Young adults who abuse amphetamines may be raising their risk of suffering a heart attack, a new study shows.

Texas researchers found that among more than 3 million 18- to 44-year- olds hospitalized in their state between 2000 and 2003, those who were abusing amphetamines were 61 percent more likely than non-users to be treated for a heart attack.

What's more, the rate of amphetamine-linked heart attacks rose by 166 percent over the 4-year study period. That compared with a 4-percent rise in cocaine-related heart attacks, the researchers report in the journal Drug and Alcohol Dependence.

"Most people aren't surprised that methamphetamines and amphetamines are bad for your health," lead researcher Dr. Arthur Westover said in a statement.

"But we are concerned because heart attacks in the young are rare and can be very debilitating or deadly," added Westover, an assistant professor of psychiatry at the University of Texas Southwestern Medical Center at Dallas.

Amphetamines stimulate the central nervous system and some are used to treat attention-deficit hyperactivity disorder, or ADHD. But they are also frequently used illegally; one potent form of amphetamine, methamphetamine, is a growing problem in many U.S. cities.

Cases of heart attack in young people have been linked to amphetamine abuse before, but the current study appears to be the first large-scale look at the epidemiology of the problem.

Westover and his colleagues used a statewide database to examine information on more than 3.1 million 18- to 44-year-olds discharged from Texas hospitals between 2000 and 2003. Overall, 11,011 of these patients (0.35 percent) were treated for a heart attack.

The database also contained information on whether a patient had been diagnosed with any type of drug-abuse problem. The researchers found that patients with a diagnosis of amphetamine abuse or dependence were at increased risk of suffering a heart attack.

Amphetamines have various effects that could precipitate a heart attack, Westover and his colleagues point out. The drugs are well known to speed up heart rate and blood pressure, but they can also trigger spasms in the heart arteries and promote blood clotting.
In people who already have "plaque" deposits in their heart arteries, amphetamines may cause a plaque to rupture, which can then lead to a heart attack.

Besides the risk to individual amphetamine users, Westover said, "we're also concerned that the number of amphetamine-related heart attacks could be increasing."

"We'd rather raise the warning flag now than later," he added. "Hopefully, we can decrease the number of people who suffer heart attacks as the result of amphetamine abuse."

SOURCE: Drug and Alcohol Dependence, July 2008.
SOURCE: Drug and Alcohol Dependence 2008
SOURCE: Reuters Health

"Methamphetamine is dangerous not only to the meth user but to society at large. It is estimated that every pound of methamphetamine produced leaves behind 5 to 7 pounds of toxic waste."

(www.streetdrugs.org)

"CHEESE" — IT'S NOT JUST FOR LUNCH ANYMORE!

Just when I think I've heard it all, all the latest ways to get high, the inventive new names for drugs, the ingenious ways kids devise to consume them, along comes another one that boggles my mind.

Here is the latest information I've found on a highly addictive, and lethal drug combination that is, according to many people in the drug addiction field, becoming as problematic as marijuana use is among young teens.

Listen carefully to what your kids say. I can't emphasize that enough. Our innocent ears do not always pick up on what our kids are really talking about. Cheese? That delicious food that goes so great with macaroni that is the #1 food choice of most young kids? I'll never be able to enjoy my weekend treat of tomato soup and a grilled cheese sandwich again without it triggering the thought of this deadly drug combo that is threatening the lives of our children.

From the Office of National Drug Control Policy — "Cheese" heroin or "starter heroin" is a combination of black tar heroin and ground up cold medicine (Tylenol PM) containing acetaminophen and diphenhydramine. The mixture is a tan powder that is snorted.

According to users, the effects of "cheese" heroin include euphoria, disorientation, lethargy, sleepiness and hunger. This combination appears to be highly addictive. Withdrawal symptoms from "cheese" heroin may begin within twelve hours of use and include headache, chills, muscle pains, muscle spasms, anxiety, agitation, disorientation and disassociation.

This mixture has been found in middle and high schools in the Dallas, Texas area and costs around $2 per hit and $10 per gram. Over the past two years, there have reportedly been approximately 20 teen deaths in the Dallas area due to "cheese" heroin. The number of arrests involving possession of "cheese" heroin in the Dallas area during the 2006–2007 school year was 146, which is an increase from approximately 90 such arrests the year before.

From Tracy Sabo, CNN.com — Parts excerpted — A cheap, highly addictive drug known as "cheese heroin" has killed 21 teenagers in the Dallas area over the past two years, and authorities say they are hoping they can stop the fad before it spreads across the nation.

A double whammy — you're getting two downers at once," says Dallas police detective Monty Moncibais. "If you take the body and you start slowing everything down, everything inside your body, eventually you're going to slow down the heart until it stops and, when it stops, you're dead."

Steve Robertson, a special agent with the Drug Enforcement Administration in Washington, says authorities are closely monitoring the use of "cheese" in Dallas.
Why should a parent outside Dallas care about what's happening there?
Robertson says it's simple: The ease of communication via the Internet and cell phones allows a drug trend to spread rapidly across the country.

"A parent in New York should be very concerned about a drug trend in Dallas, a drug trend in Kansas City, a drug trend anywhere throughout the United States," he says.

"Cheese" is not only dangerous. It's cheap. About $2 for a single hit and as little as $10 per gram. The drug can be snorted with a straw or through a ballpoint pen, authorities say. It causes drowsiness and lethargy, as well as euphoria, excessive thirst and disorientation. That is, if the user survives.

Heroin —

Back by Popular Demand!

The following two articles appeared in the Long Island Press on June 26th, 2008. I include these articles in this book because sadly they do not have a shelf life. The heroin problem is still around and in fact, is enjoying a resurgence in popularity among older teens and young adults.

Although these stories take place in Long Island, NY, (or Long Highland as reporters Robbie Woliver, Michael Martino, Jr., and Timothy Bolger say with tongues planted firmly in cheeks) the truth is these stories are taking place all over our country today. No city is immune to the lure of heroin. This is really about every city, your city, my city.

The people in these stories are real. I wish I could say they're fictional characters. But they're not. They could very well be your children or children you know or your adult next door neighbors.

These tragedies do not have to happen. If, and granted that is an enormous if, we can prevent our children from ever taking that first step down that dark path, that first drug, then I believe society has a chance to stem the tide, to truly save our children from the ravages of drugs. The key is Prevention. It is so much harder to stop doing drugs than it is to not do drugs in the first place.

It is better to say "No thank you, I don't want to ruin my life with drugs," than to say "Oh my God, what have I done? Why did I start doing drugs? I just want my life back. Please help me! I just want to be a kid again." My heart breaks when moms relate these words to me as spoken by their children. May you never have to hear them yourself.

My thanks to the reporters who so graciously granted me permission to reprint these articles in their entirety.

> *"Heroin is easier to get than alcohol. The liquor stores and bars eventually close but the heroin stores are open 24 hours a day."*
>
> **(www.drugstory.org)**

LONG HIGHLAND

They had all the proof they needed that they were fighting a real war.

Recently, two detectives from the Nassau County narcotics/vice squad went for a quick bite at a county line area bagel store. Both are seasoned veterans, having fought the darker side of suburban life for some years. Among other duties, of late, their time had been spent dealing with an increasing heroin problem in Nassau County, one they know is very real and very frightening.

Across the store, they noticed a young man sitting at a table falling asleep, or nodding off, into his lunch. Moments later, another young man exited the men's room with blood trickling down his arm. The detectives moved in to investigate. The young man snoozing in his bagel was arrested after the cops found heroin in his pocket. In the confusion, the bleeder got away.

This was in the middle of the day, in a typically white, middle-class American suburb. And it is becoming a familiar story.

Jessica* seems like the nicest girl in the world. She's soft-spoken, bright-eyed and as sweet as can be, the kind of girl you'd want your kids to hang out with.

For years, she'd find the kind of kids *she* wanted to hang out with on the streets of Levittown. That's where the former Island Trees High School student would wander to buy her heroin-from fellow students. That is, until the night her stepmother found her in bed unconscious, blue-faced, with saliva dribbling down the side of her mouth, ODed.

"I almost died," remembers Jessica.

In the hospital, she was shot with adrenaline through a needle in her heart, an instant detox. She remained in the hospital with a collapsed lung for a week, going cold turkey.

"I was convulsing and thrashing, trying to get out of my body," she recalls. "I weighed 100 pounds and eight people had to hold me down. I look back at it now and cringe. I had no concept of how I was playing with death."

She started using heroin at 15 and stayed on it for four years. Now, five years clean and 24 years old, she says, "I desire it all the time. I liked the rush and release. It was an exciting, thrilling and new experience that you just cannot feel unless you're high."

That's what authorities are up against.

In The Trenches

Going to the offices of the Nassau County Police Department Narcotics/Vice Squad (NCNVS) makes you feel like you are up to no good. There, they don't look like cops, and there's a degree of mistrust in their eyes that cannot be shaken. It is the product of dealing with liars for a living.

Detective Lt. Andrew Fal's face does not carry the lines one might expect from a cop who has been on the job almost 40 years. As the commanding officer of the NCNVS, Fal has a lot on his plate. His day consists of dealing with some of the darkest aspects of the human condition, including human trafficking, prostitution and drug dealing. He has seen the drinking age change more than once, several police commissioners and county executives come and go, and crime stats go up and down in Nassau. Nothing should surprise him, really. But recently he has been shocked by something he never thought he would see again: heroin, once again taking root as a popular drug, on LI's manicured streets.

When heroin began to show up in arrests around Nassau, especially with young people, Fal was stunned.

"I said, 'No, this can't be,'" says Fal, who remembers when heroin began to claim lives in Nassau 30 years ago. "I mean, how stupid are these kids?"

There is no denying that the drug is a big problem among kids in their late teens and early 20s, says Fal. Across Nassau and Suffolk, more and more arrests, overdoses and, most disturbingly, casual use, are related to the drug that is perhaps the most hardcore of all illicit substances.

According to Detective Lt. Peter Donohue, deputy commanding officer of the NCNVS, the numbers don't lie. In 2003 in Nassau, he says, there were 102 heroin-related arrests. Last year, there were 151-a frightening increase of almost 50 percent. But those numbers can be misleading. Many people who are arrested for petty crimes, rather than drugs, are committing them for one reason-to get more heroin.

Although Suffolk police were unable to make heroin arrest statistics available as of presstime, *The New York Times* reported 95 fatal heroin-related overdoses in 2005 in Suffolk, compared to the 47 in 2004. Rehab clinic admissions for opiate abuse from a criminal justice referral source rose in both counties, by 32 percent in Nassau and twice as much-66 percent-in Suffolk between 2000 and 2007, according to the New York State Office of Alcohol and Substance Abuse Services.

"Heroin is emerging as a threat," says Suffolk County District Attorney Tom Spota through his spokesman. "Over the past few years, a significant rise in the drug's purity coupled with a greater supply on the streets has resulted in an increase in the frequency of heroin overdoses," the spokesman added. As a result, in 2005, Suffolk County police responded by creating a special unit in the county police narcotics bureau, to track and investigate heroin overdose cases.

Detective Lt. William Burke, commanding officer of the Suffolk Police Narcotics Section, points out that there has been a shift in the heroin-abusing demographic since his rookie days three decades ago.

"When I first came on the police department, I always came across heroin junkies who were 40-year-olds. Now you will see younger kids using heroin," he says, attributing the change to the new, stronger wave of smack. He gives another reason for the resurgence: Today's heroin is cheaper.

"It's a trend that's been going on over the last several years," adds Burke. "We have issues with heroin everywhere."

"OBVIOUS AND OUT IN THE OPEN"

According to the NCNVS, the hotbed of LI's heroin community seems to be the South Shore communities of Massapequa, Bellmore, Merrick, Seaford, Wantagh, Copiague, Lindenhurst and Babylon.

But the epidemic does not stop there. Tony North Shore towns are also facing their own problems, Fal warns. Economics may play a role in why the rest of the Island may not hear of these issues on the Gold Coast.

"On the North Shore, the problem is well hidden behind money," says

Fal. "When a kid gets in trouble, [he or she] is sent off to rehab quietly."

And many teenagers and young adults do seem to be in trouble. Students at Syosset High School say that there's a pocket of seniors who have $400-a-day heroin habits. High school kids in Copiague say that their town is home to dealers who service teens. Massapequa High School students say heroin use is rampant-"obvious and out in the open"-in their school and town. At Ward Melville High School in East Setauket, the commons is called "The Pharmacy." At Sachem North, there's a part of the school openly known as "The Drugstore." Lindenhurst High School students brag that they're the "Heroin Capital of Long Island." And in Bellmore, kids from Calhoun High School say heroin is so prevalent that in some families, it's an intergenerational thing. Several sources from different towns report that some middle- and upper-class kids have junkie parents, and they steal their stash.

Most of the students and heroin users interviewed for this story warn that young heroin users aren't the stereotypical-looking strung-out junkies we know from the movies. These are white middle-class kids who pass for normal, looking sweet and typical-like Jessica-but who often suffer and die silently.

"Parents need to know that their goody-goody child could be doing heroin," says Jill*, 25, a seven-year crack and heroin user from Babylon, "and unless they pay very close attention, there are very few telltale signs until it is too late."

"Weekends and parties are the places where most of these kids use heroin," says one Syosset High School senior, who takes drugs but not heroin.

Across the board, the consensus is that the increasingly common path to heroin starts with what users call "pharm parties," where kids take whatever opiate-based prescription drugs are in their parents' medicine cabinet-Vicodin, Percocet, oxycodone-perhaps going so far as to crush the pills into a powder and sniff them. Teens who abuse prescription drugs are 12 times likelier to use heroin, according to a 2005 Columbia University study that also found that prescription drug abuse by teens tripled between 1992 and 2003.

Smackonomics

There is something very wrong when heroin is more affordable than gasoline. But, say police sources, that is exactly the situation. NCNVS's Donohue says that heroin is cheaper and easier to get than ever before.

Users agree that it does not cost much money at all to get into the game. A small bag could cost as little as $7. Once the heroin habit really begins, junkies may start to buy in "bundles," which could be as many as 11 or 12 bags, but usually an even 10. That could cost about $200 or less. The typical user buying in that quantity would get about two bundles, or 20 bags.

Fal says that the drugs are being sold primarily by neighborhood kids who start out by going to Brooklyn, Queens or the Bronx to buy heroin for themselves. As word begins to spread, they start to pick up heroin for friends. Suddenly, they are dealers.

"They find their trade expands exponentially," says Fal. "They never see themselves as dealers when they are arrested. They just think they are picking up for their friends."

"Brooklyn's the cheapest," says a Syosset High senior. This is confirmed by most of the junkies who find they have to go off the Island to buy their heroin after they graduate high school.

"It's so easy to get heroin in school," says Jessica. "When you graduate, you graduate to Brooklyn or the Bronx, and things start to get seriously dangerous."

Most heroin users remain under the radar until their addiction causes them to commit petty crimes to support the habit. At first, they're stealing from parents and friends. Then they get more desperate. When caught, if they don't have heroin on them, they could be off the hook for the drug charge.

Being caught with a small amount of heroin, say, a small bag or two, is treated as a misdemeanor possession charge. The addict could be back doing the drug in just hours-or even less.

But getting caught with multiple bags could result in an intent-to-sell charge, which is big trouble for the suspect. They could wind up in custody at the worst time: when their withdrawal begins. Then it is a completely different nightmare altogether.

Not Just Horsing Around

Heroin is a hell of drug. Few substances have its immediate addictive qualities. Heroin is derived from the poppy plant, native to Southeastern Europe and Western Asia, but now is cultivated in many other parts of the world. Cops say the majority of the heroin that makes it to LI comes from countries such as Colombia, via Mexico. A member of the opiate family, which are the most addictive drugs, heroin goes right to the brain. It's that first hit that a heroin addict will chase after, forever. It is a futile chase, as most addicts will tell you.

It's been said by junkies that heroin is better than sex. While most would probably disagree, it makes scientific sense. In the early 1970s, scientists found that the human brain has receptors that seem to welcome opiates with open arms. Morphine, heroin, opium and other similar substances affect the part of the brain that releases endorphins, those sweet, natural brain chemicals that provide a "rush."

Some have said the initial rush of heroin is like an orgasm, complete with flushed skin and heavy limbs. But as the drug begins to settle down and travel through the body, it acts like morphine, numbing and calming the nerves. The feeling is so pleasant that users want to do it again. And again-well, that is, if they don't mind vomiting every once in a while. Welcome to the Terror Dome.

"Users develop a tolerance, so you need more and more heroin to feel the euphoria that is associated with the first heroin high," says Dr. Joseph Rio, the chief toxicologist for the Nassau County Medical Examiner's office.

Consequently, the brain urges the addict to do whatever is necessary to get that high. Of course, along the way the body begins to develop a dependence, too. Rio says that, not unlike substances like tobacco, the physical hook of heroin becomes a painful, nagging feeling.

But that tolerance is phony, because it is only the brain that is getting used to the opiate effect of the drug. The body continues to take a pounding, and there is no real tolerance level to achieve. Organs like the liver and kidneys will be damaged. And once a sniffer graduates to the needle, a host of other issues present themselves, including hepatitis B and C, HIV/AIDS, abscesses from repeated punctures not being cleaned, and other infections. Once someone begins doing heroin, there really is no upside.

Fal says, though, that this dependence works to the advantage of the cops.

"Addicts don't want to get sick," says Fal. "They get what we call diarrhea of the mouth."

That is when the cops can start to break down the walls of silence built up by drug addicts.

"When we arrest addicts, they know they only have a certain amount of time before they start to sneeze, get chills, and eventually be lying on the floor in the fetal position in withdrawal," says Donohue. And don't forget the insatiable itching, parodied by non-users but feared by junkies.

And a junkie will do anything to get a fix. That desperation has led to recent arrests in both counties. Sources confirm a recent bevy of arrests in the Massapequa area, which they believe will continue to lead to more information.

Recently, a married couple was arrested for a string of robberies in Massapequa. The man and wife were robbing school-aged kids, tearing chains from the kids' necks or grabbing whatever they could to fund their heroin addiction. Beyond south Nassau, on June 25 in north Suffolk, 21-year-old Victor Chunga of Smithtown was sentenced to 35 years to life for stabbing to death 70-year-old Martha Watson in her Nesconset home last December. Chunga stabbed Watson while trying to steal heroin from her grandson, Matthew Watson, who had stopped supplying Chunga with heroin. Matthew Watson was also stabbed repeatedly, but lived.

Fighting The Fire

The problem is so alarming that Nassau Police Commissioner Lawrence Mulvey and County Executive Tom Suozzi hosted a May 8 conference organized by the Nassau County Police Department for Nassau's school administrators.

A multimedia presentation opened the eyes of school officials, for many had no idea that heroin was making such a comeback locally.

The police department announced that it was holding the meeting with school personnel from districts "located in the south corridor of Nassau County, where an increase in the use of heroin amongst teens has made a significant resurgence." And yet, many insist that the drug is not a problem within their schools.

When asked about heroin use at Massapequa High School, Massapequa Public Schools administrators responded to the *Press* with fervor.

"The Board of Education and administration have never been informed of any use of heroin within the high school by our supervisory staff," said Acting Superintendent of Schools Charles Sulc in a letter faxed and mailed to the *Press*. "Furthermore, the Nassau County Police Department has never been in contact with the Board of Education, nor any level of the high school or district's administration, regarding heroin use by Massapequa High School students."

Sulc did not return calls from the *Press*, relying only on the letter.

Robert Schilling, executive director, assessment, student data & technology services for Massapequa Public Schools, flatly denied any heroin incidents with Massapequa High School. He did, however, attend the police department's conference. So what did he do with the information gleaned from such a dramatic presentation?

The school district had no comment on that question. Neither did officials from both the Copiague and Lindenhurst school districts, according to an e-mail from their publicist, Kathy Beatty.

"We had no specific [incidents] at Massapequa High School," says Fal. "But, in general, there is a problem. And, it's a conclusion you can make, that it is in the schools.

"We are not about mincing words," Fal continues. "We made that presentation so all the school administrators knew that [heroin] could be coming. It's an emerging problem. We have to create an awareness. You can't just wait until you have a problem."

On a recent walk through downtown Park Avenue in Massapequa Park, Massapequa High School students were observed spending their newfound summer freedom hanging out on benches lining the street. When asked, one 16-year-old boy admitted to heroin use. "It's a good drug," he said, while trying to persuade passersby to purchase cigarettes for him and his friends.

At nearby Brady Park, a small, informal 18th birthday remembrance for a boy from Massapequa who died unexpectedly this past March was taking place. His friends were open about the boy's heroin use.

"Plain and simple, [Massapequa High School] has problems with dope," said the dead boy's 20-year-old friend from Levittown. The friend admitted that he himself is a former heroin user, right after the group at the table finished smoking some marijuana. "I don't think [the school district] wants to admit they have a problem," said the Levittown friend. He would know-he did heroin with the Massapequa teens.

Ask any junkie in high school, and they will probably laugh at the idea of the administration not knowing that heroin is being used by students in the school. Often, these kids do not hide the fact that they use.

Edward, now 24, took heroin while at Lindenhurst High School. He says, bluntly, "They knew who we were. It's this generation's drug of choice." This sentiment is echoed by many young heroin users.

Jessica, who once trolled the streets of Levittown for drugs as a high school student, agrees. She says, "Teachers are well aware of the heroin use. I had one girl in my English class announce to the whole class, in front of the teacher, 'I was up all night doing heroin.' I thought the teacher was going to flip out."

But Alice Andersen, a licensed social worker who serves as the drug and alcohol counselor for Levittown Division High School, says she has never seen a student with a heroin problem at the school.

"Alcohol and pot have always been the drugs of choice," she says. "We have not had one child [on heroin], or one report of heroin abuse in the school."

Ask someone who has used, though, and you get a very different answer.

"I knew I could always get heroin from a student from Levittown," says Jessica.

But it's not just administrators who disagree that heroin is becoming more prevalent. Some students do as well.

"I don't think it's really that bad-it's just certain kids," says Andrew Carroll, 17, who graduated Massapequa High School in June. The former hockey team captain, taking a quick break from his job at a local deli, described the news coverage focusing on the school as "exaggerated." Others see any trace of heroin use as something to be concerned about.

Abusing heroin leads to obvious addiction, but too often that habit will end in death. Dr. Rio explains that heroin affects the brain as it is communicating with the body. So, the brain might tell the heart to stop pumping blood, or the lungs to stop breathing. Too often, when someone who is high on heroin goes to sleep, they never wake up.

By all accounts, the heroin that is being used today is immeasurably more potent than in the past. The potency allows users to sniff heroin as opposed to shooting it at first. That is a mind trick that Fal believes gets the ball rolling in the wrong direction.

"Kids think it's no big deal if they sniff it," says Fal. "It takes the stigma away from the drug. The image of someone using a needle is not reality to them."

But no matter how it's taken, heroin use is a harsh reality. A hit of heroin that is sniffed or snorted can take up to 15 minutes to affect the brain. A subcutaneous injection-one that goes just under the skin-will make its way to the shooter's system in about 10 minutes. But an intravenous shot, one straight into the vein, is almost instant.

"We've been in a little bit of an upswing," says Kevin Leonard, clinic manager with the Suffolk County Department of Health's Division of Community Mental Hygiene. He is careful not to term the increase a trend, describing opiate abuse as "cyclical in nature," and noting that in his three decades in the rehab field, he's seen lots of ups and downs in terms of heroin use.

Meanwhile, though, Fal, Burke and the rest of the cops across the Island remain steadfast in stamping out the flare-ups before they become an inferno. Fal remains astounded that heroin use is even an issue.

"With all the technology and information at their fingertips, how could these kids do heroin?" he wonders. "I mean, heroin is not just recreational. It is highly addictive. It causes problems. It increases crime."

Fal pauses.

"And, it causes death," he says. "They just don't understand the consequences."

-With additional reporting

by Heather Burian

*Not their real names.

Update to Long Highland story from Robbie Woliver Editor-In-Chief Long Island Press: Principal Jim Nolan of Sachem North High School in Ronkonkoma, a school also mentioned in the "Long *High-land*" story, contacted us unsolicited and proactively after reading the story, to find out how, in any way, he could help his students."

> "The human mind is capable of excitement without the application of gross and violent stimulants; and he must have a very faint perception of its beauty and dignity who does not know this."
>
> **William Wordsworth, poet**

It is not heroin or cocaine that makes one an addict, it is the need to escape from a harsh reality. There are more television addicts, more baseball and football addicts, more movie addicts, and certainly more alcohol addicts in this country than there are narcotics addicts."

Shirley Chisholm, congresswoman, educator

Junk Bonds

As Their Lives Disintegrate (And Are Occasionally Rebuilt), Long Island Heroin Users Search For The Next High

Carol Whelan, a nurse, sits on her couch in her cramped, middle-class Cape home in Lindenhurst, occupied by a laughing parrot, two dogs and a monkey. She shakes her head sadly. "The truth is," she says, "I'm getting tired of going to so many funerals of young people."

The young people she is talking about are her son Edward's friends. They were around his age, 24, when they died, and the death count is now about 10. The most recent was the worst-Thomas, Edward's best friend.

And what are they dying from? Heroin.

Edward is an imposing young man, 6-foot-2-inches tall, 195 pounds, a good-looking Penn Jillette with long hair in a partial ponytail and one of those great giant-dimpled smiles that lights up the room. That's not the only thing that's lit up in Edward's basement studio on this unusually hot June evening, where several of his friends are gathering. There's also Ricky and Lorraine, a 27-year-old married couple from Bellmore. They are junkies and they have just gotten high.

Edward, too, has been on heroin. That is, until this past April, a month after Thomas ODed.

"I just stopped," he says. "In honor of [Thomas]."

Sitting amongst the heavy metal posters, drum sets, electric keyboards and assorted other instruments where Edward's heavy metal band InRed practices, are Jill, 25, and Ryan, 25-two of Edward's friends who also were heroin users, but who have since gone to rehab and are currently sober. Jill and Ryan have been clean since January of this year, and Ryan has been out of rehab since early May. Ryan came close to using heroin a week and a half ago, but a friend stopped him, and Ryan is very thankful his friend did that.

"It's a day-to-day struggle," admits Ryan, who looks like the clean-cut jock-next-door.

While Ryan and Jill discuss their successes, Ricky, with an almost clichéd hangdog look, is nodding out near his wife, who has such a sad aura about her it is palpable. When showing the needle marks on her black-and-blue arms, the scars of recent cuttings are also obvious. Ricky looks helpless as she shows her bruised arms-even though he does help shoot his wife's battered veins with heroin.

Tonight Ricky-who seems like he might once have been a sharp, interesting young man-is, shortly after shooting heroin, zombie-like. Edward, Jill and Ryan seem absolutely radiant, compared to him. He is their past.

"I can end any time I want," says Ricky, obviously not believing his own empty words. Ricky, Edward says, is unusual. "He can stop for a day and be OK. That's very hard to do," Edward says, almost in awe of his slumped-over, droopy-eyed, sallow friend. OK is a relative term here.

Jill and Ryan, who are not too far past that life themselves, agree. Jill, for example, was shooting up heroin several times a day. And that was just to bring her down from the crack cocaine she was smoking.

"I had a 95 average in high school," she says, wistfully describing her past. "I had a lot of dreams, but now I just make f**king $7.50 an hour in Waldbaum's." Unlike the others in this group, Jill started drugs late, at age 18. Coke was her drug of choice, and she had been an addict for close to seven years, first taking ecstasy, then snorting coke and then smoking crack and finally shooting heroin to come down from the coke and crack. She started late, but she made up for it big time.

She was shooting up all day, but no longer getting high, so she needed more and more. For a while she worked three jobs and says she kept up her appearance, but that all came to an abrupt end. She lost about 30 pounds (as did Ryan when he was using) and fell to 80 pounds. She now weighs a healthy 110 pounds and looks fit. She also collapsed a vein and now can't get blood taken from the arm.

The wake-up call? There were several. ODing was a biggie. "I almost died," she says. "My heart stopped." At this point her skin was yellow, she had black eyes and her back teeth fell out. She also couldn't breathe. "The doctor told me I had such a large hole in my nose [from snorting drugs] that it would kill me," she recalls

So she stopped snorting. And she started injecting.

Jill, who never smoked pot, says she was oblivious to the degeneration of her circle of junkie friends. "They had no teeth. They were dirty like bums," she says in retrospect.

Remember, while these users are now in their 20s, they all started using drugs as teens, some as young as preteens.

It was rampant in school, they all say. "You can count the people who aren't on heroin," says Edward, "as opposed to the ones who are." And Lindenhurst, they all say, is "the heroin capital of Long Island." That is, until Bellmore and Massapequa and Copaigue and Levittown and countless other towns come up.

"It's wherever you go, and the kids are getting younger and younger," says Edward, who attended Lindenhurst High School (partly at the Alternative Learning Center [ALC]). "We'd smoke weed in the class-room. In ninth grade, kids would have coke and heroin on the table in the classroom.

"A lot of kids from the high school and ALC would get sent away for a year or so, their drug problem would be so bad," Edward says. His best friend Thomas was one of those kids.

Why heroin?

"It's a social drug, and everyone was doing it," says Edward, who, like many of his friends, first began experimenting with drugs at age 11.

He started heroin when he was 14. His entire crowd was doing it. (There are some, who, 10 years later, are still on heroin.) It was cheap and very easy to get. Their stories are similar-they started by sniffing it and eventually turned to shooting it.

"It makes you not care what anyone says. It makes you an asshole," he says. "But I liked the feeling. It was amazing."

There is no stigma, nor a badge of honor. It's just what everybody does. No big deal.

"It was cheaper than marijuana, coke, pills and alcohol, and one $10 bag would do the trick," says Jill. The coke high is only 20 minutes. Heroin would last longer, until the tolerance would build.

And where are the parents in all this? Jill says her parents "thought something was up. It was obvious, I wasn't holding down a job, I wasn't going to school.

"When my mom would go to work, I would shoot up and it would last two to three hours and then I'd have to get high again. I had to get high two or three times a day.

"I'm getting sick just talking about it," she says.

"Toward the end, I felt like I was tripping out. I was having anxiety attacks. I was hot, cold, throwing up, very emotional. I kept trying to leave signs, leaving needles around, stuff like that."

Jill's mother, who had been addicted to cocaine herself, finally said, "That's it. I know something's up. I want to take you to a funeral home. I want you to see your funeral. I don't want to find you dead." Jill's uncle OD'd and her brother is a recovering addict.

Jill: "It was disgusting. You felt dirty no matter what you'd do. You lied to everyone. Drugs ruined my life."

So she got clean. "I took a long hard look," she says, starting to cry. But it's not easy.

She is now in a drug and alcohol program three to four days a week.

"Sometimes when I get frustrated and think about my shitty job, I ask myself, 'What am I clean for?' I know it takes a year to get really clean. But I smile again now. My family is trusting me again, and my friends are trusting me again."

At this point, Edward's cell phone rings, and he tells Jill that it's a friend of hers. Jill gets in an animated discussion with her friend, who informs her that Jill's mother is frantically searching for her, angrily saying things like, "I know she's up to no good. I know what she's doing. I know she's sneaking around."

"Fuck that," Jill says, "I told her where I was going," and with that she calls her mother and angrily reminds her that she is being interviewed for a newspaper story.

"I have no car. No phone. I live in a cubicle with no door, no privacy," she says. "They are treating me like I am 16.

"There are so many things I could have done with my life," Jill says.

Edward's situation is a little different. His parents are more trusting. They were very supportive when he came to them last January and told them that he was a junkie.

"I suspected something," says his mother, who is a methadone nurse.

"It's better when you have their support," says Edward, the soft-spoken rocker.

Part of why so many young people are junkies is the ease with which they can obtain the heroin, says Edward. "We'd go to [the dealer's] house and there would be cars lined up-sometimes 10 cars on each block. We had to wait hours almost every day." Ryan laughs at the memory. What they don't address is the danger inherent in these deals. These dealers, who sometimes have their much younger siblings deliver the goods, are dead serious, and they have the firearms to prove it.

But these dangers are of no significance to a junkie, when caught up in heroin's web. "Everyone seems to be doing it," says Edward. "In high school it seemed like 80 percent of the kids were doing it."

"And then there's the environment," Ryan adds. "Every commercial says, 'Take this pill.' Society is feeding you with drugs and saying, 'This will solve this problem.'"

What's the effect of school programs like DARE? These heroin users say, for them, the programs did more harm than good.

"They lied to us about marijuana, so we didn't believe them about heroin," says Edward.

And then there's the cheap cost. "I couldn't afford weed and alcohol," says Edward. "Heroin was a snap: $10 a bag."

But that $10 has a greater cost.

Married to the drug

Ricky and Lorraine have been married for three years. Ricky has been sniffing heroin for about six months, and has been shooting up for the past six weeks. "You need more when you're sniffing it and it's more expensive," he explains.

Ricky's reason for using heroin is somewhat startling. "I install carpets," he says, "and I am in pain a lot. Tylenol will do nothing."

That's the problem. Heroin is no big deal.

"It takes away the pain," Ricky says. "It takes away the physical muscle pain and the mental anguish. You're just not aware of anything. I want to stop doing it. I am trying to get off it now. I know it's bad. The addiction is just uncontrollable."

Jill shakes her head, and responds, "When you're on it you always make plans to quit. It's not that easy."

Lorraine, slouched over as she speaks, wears a pretty brown ribbon in her hair, making her seem girlish and innocent. But that couldn't be further from the truth. She's been on opiates for four years, and was hooked on morphine. She has been doing drugs since she was 13.

"Heroin addicts don't last very long...a year," says Lorraine, who has been doing heroin for the past seven months. She's been shooting up for the past six weeks.

"I can't imagine a good life," she says, head down, about her future. What about life with each other now? "[Ricky] seems a little more zombielike, secretive, when he uses [heroin]," she explains. "I don't believe a word he says. He does six bags, two needles, sometimes before he even really wakes up."

Besides mistrust, there is no intimacy amongst junkies. Ricky, who started drugs at 14, says, "We don't think about sex. It's not an option."

"We know it's bad," says his wife Lorraine. "We just encourage each other. We say, 'This is ridiculous, we have to stop.' Then the other one says, 'You want to get high?' We're never in agreement."

"I don't care if I do it by myself. I don't really care. I'll do it in a parking lot, on the side of the road," Ricky says.

"Are you afraid of being arrested?" he's asked. He looks back with a blank stare.

"Maybe that would be good," someone adds.

"Our families are really concerned," Lorraine says dead-eyed, with no emotion.

Quittin' Time

How do you get the strength to quit?

"You have to be tired of the life, because you'll never get tired of the feeling," says Edward.

Ryan, who's been friends with Edward since kindergarten, has been on drugs since his early teens. He started off with pain killers, Vicodin, OxyContin, and then moved to heroin a year ago, "because it was cheaper," he says. "You'd get higher and it was a cleaner high." He entered rehab in January of this year and got out on May 2.

All five say they stole from parents and friends to support their habit. Some worked.

"Our money situation is hard," complains Lorraine, in the same tone she would use to say she was wearing a ribbon in her hair. Of course it's hard; there are two junkies who need to satisfy their addictions.

"I remember what that is like," says Ryan. "I would have rather taken $80 and spent it on drugs than eat three meals. I always said, 'I don't have a problem.' Just like Ricky is doing now. I remember coming here [Edward's house], puking. I didn't give a shit."

Ryan returns to the recent incident, when he almost used again. "After all the effort I put into it, it would hurt my family," he says. "They were so proud of me. One of the best feelings was finishing the program."

Jill looks at Ricky and tells him he's beginning to look like a junkie.

"What does a junkie look like?" he asks. "Your skin is yellowish," she responds. "It's the way you carry yourself. Your facial structure. It changes from weight loss. You look like one," she reiterates.

"Have you noticed the changes in him?" Lorraine is asked.

"I guess," Lorraine says.

Jill shakes her head. She's been there.

Edward knows there's no talking sense to the two. They need something to scare them, or to inspire them.

An inspiration like Thomas.

Thomas died from a heroin overdose on March 5, 2008. Edward stopped shooting heroin a month later.

"He promised me he would never die," says Edward about the friend he had known since they were both 8. "He e-mailed me the day before he died, saying that."

Two weeks after the gathering in Edward's basement, Jill was in a local Applebee's, where she noticed the clientele staring at a particular table where a couple was sitting "facedown in their food." It was Ricky and Lorraine.

At press time, Edward notified us that he had just learned that two more friends died of ODs. He called back soon after to also inform us that Ricky and Lorraine had been arrested for possession. They scored some heroin and on the way home, Lorraine suggested they shoot up in an abandoned parking lot in Bellmore, close to where they live. Ricky suggested they go home and do it. Lorraine won out, and they quickly were discovered by a cop on patrol. Lorraine is out on $2,500 bail but Ricky remains in jail. Ricky says that this is a good thing, and he hopes it will help him clean up.

Some of the names used in this story have been changed.

By: Robbie Woliver

rwoliver@ longislandpress.com

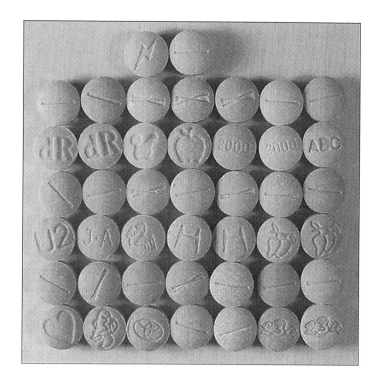

Picture courtesy of the DEA

An Example of Ecstasy

Heather's Story

An Inspiring Tale of Courage and Hope

I was addicted to drugs from the time I was fifteen years old to thirty-three years old. I have five years in recovery now. No one, including myself, thought I would ever get off drugs. As they said in the treatment program where I lived for six months, "the money was not on me that I would make it." But I did make it. Against all odds, I am alive today. Not only am I alive, but I am truly happy most of the time. My friends and family are in my life. I have an amazing career working in a treatment center where I help family members get their loved ones treatment. I have a car, an apartment, and a dog that I love more than I ever thought imaginable. And I write! I take a class once a week where I turn my life experiences into stories. These might seem like small things – things that I should take for granted because this is what most people are supposed to have. But I don't take it for granted, not for one second. The fact that I have this life today is a miracle. You see, not only was I a drug addict, but I was addicted to heroin, and a chronic overdoser. I never set out to overdose. But I did – approximately twenty times. I was revived with naloxone (the antidote to an opiate overdose), with rescue breathing, and more than once 911 had to be called.

In the beginning, it was all about surviving my family life. When I was in my early teens, my mom moved in with a Vietnam Vet who was also an alcoholic. Due to untreated Post Traumatic Stress Disorder and alcoholic drinking, he was violent and caused a lot of terror and anxiety in our house. Many people I meet in recovery come from similar backgrounds. Some of us blame our parents and some of us don't. I love my mom and know she did the best she could. But I also know that being raised in an extremely violent household affected me. By the time I discovered the tranquilizers in my mom's medicine cabinet, I was already looking for an effective means of escape. With that first pill, for the first time in my life, I felt at peace and able to survive the violence and madness in my home without committing suicide.

If I had a feeling, any feeling, I would use drugs in order to minimize it. By the time I started using heroin, my main goal was to anesthetize myself because at that point I was always in so much pain. What led to my frequent overdosing was always pretty much the same. A lethal combination of drugs in a quantity larger than my body could handle. Like many addicts, I used whatever drugs I could get my hands on and always used as much as possible. Consequently, my tolerance was quite high causing me to use more and more.

There are a million horrible things about an overdose, but looking back, the worst part is this: the person who suffers the most at the time of an overdose is never the person overdosing. The person overdosing is unconscious, blissfully unaware of the panic and hysteria going on around them. Of all the times I overdosed, I never once thought to get help. I am sure people suggested it to me, in fact I remember people insisting that I get help. One time, I woke up in the emergency room and was told by the doctor that I was lucky to be alive and unless I quit using, I would end up in a place far worse than the ER, namely the morgue. His warning did not faze me. I was humiliated because my friends were worried that I would die, but the need to use drugs was stronger, and as soon as they released me from the hospital, I went back to where I was before. I wish I could say that after my last overdose I "saw the light." But by the end, my drug use was so out of control and I was so full of despair, death seemed like the least of my problems. Every day was about getting more drugs. Like a lot of women I had to trade sex for drugs. I did all the things I said I would never do. I hated myself and everyone around me. I did not care that I was covered in bruises and that my hair was falling out. I did not care that my arms were scarred with track marks. Despite all this insanity, I knew I was going to die if I kept going. Either someone was going to kill me out on the streets or I was going to overdose again and not survive like my best friend, girlfriend, and countless acquaintances.

I feel it's important to mention here that even though I was strung out for those eighteen years, I did a lot of amazing things. I graduated from college with honors and was the only one in my family to go to college. I married the love of my life. I helped raise a boy born with HIV after his mother, a close friend of mine, died of AIDS. I also co-founded an HIV prevention program for drug users where I served as director for 13 years.

I don't know how I was able to hold it together so well in the first half of my drug using experience. Somehow, I was able to balance all the "normal" things I was doing in my life with the heroin addiction. Towards the end, however, I was completely consumed by drugs. But even then, there was still a small part of me that wanted to live. It was this part of me that went to my first Narcotics Anonymous meeting. Here I ran into someone I knew from my time working in the HIV prevention center, and who I trusted enough to ask for help. By some complete miracle he was able to get me into treatment right away. Because I now work in the treatment industry, I know what an extraordinary thing that was. Most addicts can't get help when they need it unless they have the financial means to pay for it. Like most addicts I didn't have any money, but was able to get help despite this fact, and am alive today because of it.

Believe it or not, entering treatment was the most difficult thing I have ever done in my life; infinitely harder than being strung-out. Once the drugs left my system, I felt as if I couldn't breathe. Living without drugs for someone who has used them their whole lives feels the way I imagine a fish out of water would feel. I was consumed with panic and felt like I was going to die every minute of every day. But the longer I stayed in the treatment program and let the people who worked there love me, the easier it got. They taught me the importance of reaching out for help by getting a sponsor and working the twelve steps of Narcotics Anonymous. They taught me that I could survive feelings, no matter how big or small, if I share them with someone else who has been where I have been. I learned what it means to be in the "flow of life": to have a job, pay my rent, walk my dog - all the seemingly mundane things that for someone like me have become the source of an incredible sense of accomplishment and serenity.

I am clearly not the same person I was five years ago. I am full of light. I laugh and I smile. I am not my pain and my past. My childhood and the ensuing years of addiction do not define me. I was lucky to get a second chance at a life that I never dreamed was possible. In a way I am grateful for these past experiences, and have come to terms with it, as the lessons I learned in the process are what allows me to be of help to other addicts in recovery.

> *"Our greatest glory is not in never falling but in rising every time we fall."*
>
> **Confucius**

PARENT'S PLEDGE

I am your loving parent, who will always be available to talk to you AND to listen to you especially when you have something that you feel is important to bring to my attention.

I will not judge you. I will remember that you are my child and therefore my responsibility.

I will listen to you with love and patience.

I will set rules for you because I love you.

I will always speak openly and honestly to you about drugs. I will not lie.

I will be strong and ensure that you don't ruin your future by doing drugs today.

I will understand that there will be times when you will not want to obey the rules but I will remain strong and enforce them because I love you and I care about you and your future.

I will take your views and feelings into consideration when setting down rules but as your parent, I will have the final say.

I will do my best to ensure that you hang around with other kids who are not doing drugs.

I will speak to the parents of your friends to see if we have the same views on drugs.

I will keep track of what websites you visit, your social networking sites, if I feel there is cause to do so. I will not invade your privacy unless I suspect there is a good reason to do so.

I will set aside time for us to do fun things, to enjoy our time together, realizing that childhood slips by all too quickly and we can't get it back.

Signed_____

"People who drink to drown their sorrow should be told that sorrow knows how to swim."

Ann Landers, newspaper columnist

CHILD'S PLEDGE

I will respect that I am your child and know that you love me and don't want me to do anything that will destroy my chances for a happy life.

I will be open and honest with you about drugs. I will let you know of any temptations that are causing me concern. I will not lie.

I will let you know if I ever give in to peer pressure and do any kind of drug. No matter how upset I know you may be, I will tell you right away because I know you will work with me to keep me drug-free. I realize that alcohol is also a drug.

I understand that I am a child and my brain is still forming and changing, and drugs can have a negative impact on my brain. I want to give my brain a chance to fully develop.

I don't want to ruin my present or my future by doing drugs. I will try to be strong and resist peer pressure to do so and I feel this can be accomplished by knowing that I can always turn to you, my parent, to help me stay drug-free.

I understand that you set rules for me out of love, not punishment. I am a teen and there will be times when I will resist your rules but I will respect them and abide by them knowing that these rules are in place to protect me.

I will expect you not to betray my confidence unless it is for the greater good.

I will read and learn about the latest drugs so that I can be forewarned and forearmed with the knowledge to help me stay drug-free and alive.

I will talk to my friends openly and honestly letting them know that I do not wish to ruin my present or my future by doing drugs.

I will expect you to be drug-free also. Together we can help each other and work toward a happy, safe, and productive future.

I will speak to you about my internet usage, my websites, my social networking sites.

I will do everything I can not to be a victim of an internet predator, realizing one of the best ways to prevent such trouble, is to confide in you about my activities.

Signed_____

"...joy and sorrow are inseparable...together they come and when one sits alone with you...remember that the other is asleep upon your bed."
Kahlil Gibran

CRIME? AND PUNISHMENT

A LOOK AT THE INCARCERATION OF DRUG-ADDICTED PEOPLE IN AMERICA

It is the opinion of the author of this book and her husband, that addicted people need Treatment, not Punishment.

We're not addressing the crimes committed by the dealers and purveyors of drugs in America, rather our focus is aimed at the drug users who have not committed violent crimes, but are languishing in our jails and prisons along with violent offenders.

We do not incarcerate alcoholics in this country (unless they commit a crime such as felony DUI or some other crime while under the influence) so why do we incarcerate drug addicted people?

It is our opinion that drug addicted people should be treated for their disease and not punished for it. Putting people in jail or prison for using drugs is not, in our opinion, the answer. Our government spends an enormous amount of money on keeping addicted people behind bars. We believe the addicted person and our nation as a whole would be better served by spending taxpayers' money on long-term addiction treatment centers.

There are many websites dedicated to reform of the criminal justice system. Due to space constraints, only a few have been selected for inclusion in this book. An internet search will yield many more results.

The following is reprinted with permission from the **November Coalition.**

Upon entering the new millennium, our nation marked the end of the most punishing decade in our people's history. More people began a prison or a jail term in the United States during the '90s than any other decade on record. There are now over two million incarcerated in the country often called "The Land of the Free."

It is no secret that punitive drug laws fuel this terrible rush to imprisonment. By studying drug law convictions over the past twenty years, researchers have produced alarming figures. The number of people sent to jail or prison for drug law violations increased more than tenfold. One in four prisoners in the United States is serving time for a drug law violation. In the federal system, these people make up 55% of the prison population.

Prison punishment increased dramatically with laws in the mid 1980's -- laws that created Mandatory Minimum sentencing, the US Sentencing Guidelines, and abolished parole. Today the Sentencing Guidelines are advisory, but those sentenced before 2004 are unlikely to be granted any retroactive relief.

For more information – (www.november.org)

"Life is like a game of cards. The hand that is dealt you represents determinism; the way you play it is free will."

Jawaharal Nehru

The following excerpt is courtesy of

The Sentencing Project
Research and Advocacy for Reform

A 25-Year Quagmire:

The War on Drugs and Its Impact on American Society

By Marc Mauer, Executive Director, and Ryan S. King, Policy Analyst, of The Sentencing Project

Drug Treatment Is More Cost Effective Than Mandatory Sentencing - A series of studies in recent years have demonstrated that drug treatment – both within and outside of the criminal justice system – is more cost-effective in controlling drug abuse and crime than continued expansion of the prison system. An evaluation of drug court programming found a reduction in drug use and criminal offending and cost savings relative to incarceration. [47]

• A recent analysis of substance abuse treatment programs in California concluded that every dollar spent on substance abuse treatment resulted in a savings of seven dollars in reduced crime and increased earnings. [48] A RAND analysis of these issues concluded that whereas spending $1 million to expand the use of mandatory sentencing for drug offenders would reduce drug consumption nationally by 13 kilograms, spending the same sum on treatment would reduce consumption almost eight times as much, or by 100 kilograms. [49] Similarly, expanding the use of treatment was estimated to reduce drug related crime up to 15 times as much as mandatory sentencing. [50] Moreover, there is some evidence that simply warehousing individuals in prison may have a criminogenic effect, as research has found higher rates of recidivism for persons sentenced to prison rather than probation. [51]

● Among individuals who are incarcerated, studies of drug treatment in prisons have also concluded that treatment significantly reduces recidivism. One of the oldest such programs is the Stay'n Out program in New York State, established in 1977 as a prison-based therapeutic community. Evaluations of the program have found that 27% of its male graduates are rearrested after parole, compared with 40% of inmates who received no treatment or only counseling. [52] Women's re-arrest rates were generally lower than for men.

● 47 Steven Belenko, Research on Drug Courts: A Critical Review 2001 Update, The National Center on

● Addiction and Substance Abuse at Columbia University, June 2001.

● 48 Susan L. Ettner, David Huang, Elizabeth Evans, Danielle Rose Ash, Mary Hardy, Mickel Jourabchi, and

● Yih-Ing Hser, "Benefit-Cost in the California Treatment Outcome Project: Does Substance Abuse Treatment

● 'Pay for Itself,'" Health Services Research, Vol, 41, (1), 192-213, 2006.

● 49 Jonathan P. Caulkins, C. Peter Rydell, William Schwabe, and James Chiesa, Mandatory Minimum Drug

● Sentences: Throwing Away the Key or the Taxpayers' Money?, RAND, 1997, at xvii-xviii.

● 50 Ibid

● 51 Cassia Spohn and David Holleran, "The Effect of Imprisonment on Recidivism Rates of Felony Offenders:

● A Focus on Drug Offenders," Criminology, Vol. 40, (2), 329-357, 2002.

For more information –(www.sentencingproject.org)

Remembering our Child

One final thought on grief and remembrance. When someone loses a child, others don't know what to say or do, even close family members struggle with this dilemma. So they take the Occam's Razor approach – do whatever is the simplest, and quite often that is to do nothing.

People often choose to say nothing, not out of disrespect or because they don't care. I believe they do care but just don't know what to say to us. Many people are afraid to broach the subject of our child's death, because they think it will make us sad. We are already sad! Nothing you can say or do will make us sadder.

But by ignoring our child, by not mentioning his/her name it is as though he or she never existed. This hurts. If you knew my child, a nice remembrance of him would be so appreciated. What mother does not want to talk about her child? Just because a child is deceased does not mean that we don't want to talk about them, or hear their name.

We think of our deceased child constantly. He/she live on in our hearts and minds. While we're looking at you and exchanging pleasantries, you can be sure that our child's memory is only a heartbeat away. So please mention our child to us. If you have a funny anecdote to share, by all means please do. Perhaps it's something we hadn't heard of before. Don't hold back. If our child did a kindness for you please tell us. It goes without saying of course that we wouldn't want to hear anything negative about our child but something nice will make us feel so good.

Please don't tell us that our child is better off, that he's in heaven. We want our child here with us! We know that you mean well but we feel that our child's place is here with us.

Please don't compare our child's death to another's death. The fact remains that our child is gone. No matter how he/she died, they're gone. That is the bottom line. Just offer a simple heartfelt condolence.

Please don't try to comfort us with words of admonition – "there now, don't cry." We'd rather not cry but sometimes it can't be helped so please allow us to give in to our tears. Tears can be healing.

Please understand that we will never be the same person that you once knew. Some of us are stronger than others and can deal with the heartache better. Some of us are very good at putting on The Mask and concealing our pain from you. We will laugh again and even enjoy life again but we will never be the same person. How could we be? A significant part of our heart is missing.

Please don't tell us that it's been X amount of weeks or months or even years and that we should be over it by now. We will never be over it. We will learn to cope but we will never be over it. Again, how could we be? There is no official time limit on mourning.

If you know my child's birthday or remember the anniversary of his/her death, a phone call would be appreciated to let me know you're thinking of me. We're a bit needier than we used to be. Grief does that to a person.

"First say to yourself what you would be; and then do what you have to do".

Epictetus, Greek philosopher

Section 2

On the following pages is a reprint from my first book - I Am Your Disease (The Many Faces of Addiction).

The narrative is compelling and explains what a stranglehold drugs have on people's brains. I wanted to include it in this book also.

The narrative is reprinted with the kind permission of Heiko Ganzer, LCSW-R, CASAC, CH of Phoenix Psychotherapy, who was my co-author on that book.

Heiko made a composite of many of his patients and combined them into one "person" – the "disease" who speaks to you and explains why it is so difficult to overcome addiction.

It is a brutally honest and bone-chilling description of addiction that everyone should read.

Addiction is a brain disease that can be treated. If you will give 100% to your recovery every hour of every day, you can beat the Addiction Monster. People have done it! You can too!

But the Monster is a formidable foe. He waits for you to let your guard down and then he pounces. Read the narrative to see what kind of enemy you face and heed the words of Winston Churchill: "Never, never, never, never give up!"

"Success is not final, failure is not fatal;
it is the courage to continue that counts."

Sir Winston Churchill

Picture courtesy of the DEA

An example of blotter acid

"I AM YOUR DISEASE"
BY: THE ANONYMOUS ADDICT

(Written by Heiko Ganzer, LCSW-R, CASAC CH)

Well, hello there! I cannot believe I have really been talked into do-ing this: Telling you about myself (which obviously you as clients either don't know, or won't accept). I am going to let you know how I operate; what my strategies are, how I win, (and I love to win!).

My initial reaction was—Why should I disclose them to you? After thinking it over, it came to me that as usual, many people will read this and not consider this information anyway, so I have nothing to lose. I mean, what the heck. Why shouldn't I divulge this stuff— who's really gonna pay attention? After all, this information has been available for many years and only a few gave a damn about it. Heck, many people, even after reading this, will still foolishly continue to take me on "their" way (how this makes me chuckle).

AA/NA/GA people try to tell them things; they won't accept it. Pro-fessional counselors tell them these things; they won't accept it, but OK, you want to hear the truth directly from the horse's mouth? Read on. They teach you that I am a disease. (I snicker because many people won't even accept that!). People fail to strongly im-press upon you what kind of disease you are up against. Words like progressive, and insidious have little impact on you so let me tell you what I'm all about—I AM YOUR DEADLIEST ENEMY!

I make AIDS look minuscule compared with the devastation I have caused and intend to continue to impact on humanity. I conduct my business of mutilation and destruction in a very business-like, highly productive, orderly manner that results in me being extremely suc-cessful! I have an insatiable desire to torture, maim and destroy. I am totally vicious! I am brutal! I have perfected my skills of deception to an art form!

Early on, in the beginning of my attack on you, I can make myself almost invisible. I take you down ever so slowly and skillfully at first because I sure as heck don't want you to become aware of me. That might frighten you away.

I am the Master of Manipulation! As my progression becomes more visible, I most emphatically am not going to let your frustration and anger be directed at me. No, no, no! I tell you it's the job, it's your spouse, and it's the kids. God forbid you should ever wise-up that it's ME. So I have you lash out at the only people who really care about you.

How I revel as I see you thrashing about throwing powder-puff punches at the world. I continually whisper outright lies in your ear and incredibly, you buy right into them. Remember when I told you "THIS TIME IT WILL BE ALRIGHT!" or "SURE YOU WENT OVERBOARD IN THE PAST, BUT THAT WON'T HAPPEN AGAIN" and my all-time classic—"YOU CAN DO IT YOUR WAY. YOU DON'T NEED ANY HELP!" Each time I lie to you, and you listen to me, I betray you. Look at your track record chump! My paramount reason for being on this earth is to make certain you never achieve your full potential or enjoy the things you deserve.

I see you start project after project, but I keep you from completing them so you rarely ever enjoy a feeling of accomplishment. I keep you chasing two rabbits at the same time and grin as I watch your dreams of tomorrow become unfulfilled promises of yesterday.

With the young I damage your potential, destroy your initiative. What pleasure I get from stunting your emotional growth, and converting you into a "never-wuz." With older people I remove the enjoyment of your autumn years, and make you into a "has-been." I adore screwing up parents. Instead of you moving forward with your lives, I suck you dry with worry and concern about the fate of your kids. In the face of all logic, reasoning and just plain common sense, Mr./Mrs. Compulsivity, you keep listening to me, and your reward for foolishly doing this is that I BETRAY YOU AGAIN, AND AGAIN, AND AGAIN!

Beginning to get the picture, Pal? I'm not exactly what you would call Mr. Nice Guy! I am a high-tech conversationalist! I just love to convert beautiful, sensitive, caring productive people into self-centered, omnipotent blood-sucking leeches who day-by-day drain their loved ones emotionally, physically, and financially. I give you selective hearing; so you hear only what I want you to hear! I give you tunnel vision; so you see what I want you to see! I roundly applaud myself as you begin to stumble through life as I prevent you from hearing and growing. How you delight me as you continually permit me to twist your thinking! By the way, pal-o-mine, I not only get a big boot out of messing you up, I am without peer when it comes to wrecking everyone who cares about you and whom you care about.

I convince you, of course, that you are only hurting yourself, no one else! As things begin getting a little tackier (that's called PROGRESSION), and unbelievably you still listen to me, I advance more rapidly within you. I cheer you on as you make emotional yo-yo's out of those who still stand at your side. Of course, you mean all those wonderful promises you make to them like "NO MORE, NEVER AGAIN," etc.

I make damn sure you never carry them out by enticing you to have just one card game, one drink, one joint, one line, or just make one little old bet. You'd better believe I don't want you wising up to the fact that I am breaking the spirit of the other people in your life; that I am causing them TEN TIMES the amount of pain and sorrow that I'm dishing out to you.

Under my influence—I grin when you say things you would not have said, I smile softly as you begin not doing things you should. I chuckle as I witness you doing things you never would have done, and I let out a real belly laugh as you begin doing unthinkable things that inflict horrible pain on those you love which now cause you even higher levels of guilt, remorse, and shame. I become ecstatic every time I witness those tears running down the faces of defenseless individuals and children who you are threatening and terrorizing (your very own spouse and kids).

I must admit I am thrilled to my toes as I rip the very life out of the people around you. Get a load of this—the target that gives me the greatest satisfaction in destroying is YOUR KIDS! I am delighted by every opportunity to keep getting them so upset and off balance by what is going on that they do not stand a chance of growing up without being severely scarred. Look at the millions, yes millions, of untreated ACOA's ACOG's, I've got romping around this country all screwed up! How I chuckle when you say "YOU'LL DIE" IF YOU DRINK, BET OR USE AGAIN! First of all you know damn well you don't really believe that, (just look at your past track record).

I do not kill people; well, sometimes I do, but when that happens it really ticks me off; obviously I socked it to that person too hard. Heck, when they die, the games are over and I've got to find a new CHUMP to take their place. Hey baby, I'd rather keep playing with them; destroy them a little at a time. No, I do my damnedest not to kill you since I want you to live—miserably, wretchedly, horribly!

One way I get my jollies is from being the world's greatest collector. Didn't know that, did you Pal? Got a warehouse the size of Africa! I happily take things away from you that rightfully belong to you. These are things that you have worked hard for, earned, and deserve. I laugh all the time; I rob you of them and store them so I can enjoy my thievery when things get a little dull.

See, there's John's RESPECT over there; and Mary's MORALITY. That's what's left of Frank's HONOR, look at this, what a blast I had ripping away Helen's INTEGRITY, and did I ever have a ball taking away young Bob's ENTHUSIASM.

How I savor fondling these trophies from my past and present robberies. Hey, get a load of all those jobs over there, how sweet it was grabbing them, and how about that pile of previously good marriages? Had a ball destroying them. Down there in that pit is where I keep active people's SELF-ESTEEM. There's Don's FREEDOM (laughed like heck when they put him in the slammer). This pile of rubble makes me just shiver with ecstasy, don't you recognize it? It used to be people's CREDIBILITY. And here sweetheart is my most prized stolen possession. Yep that big steel cage is full of thousands of broken people, what a fantastic sight all of them stumbling around! Know what I stole from them? THEMSELVES. Certainly one of my award-winning traits is to steal away YOU! I have absolutely perfected my techniques for causing the process of self-abandonment. What I excel most at is taking you away from YOU!

I'm also the unequaled master at converting things; early on I convert you into a procrastinator thus letting you build up unnecessary tension, and stress. I adore converting warm, caring people into self-centered, omnipotent jackasses, and bright, intelligent people into bumbling, fourteen carat idiots. I am the absolute Champion of Deception! I get one heck of a bang doing my Muhammed Ali "ROPA-DOPA" routine on you. I make believe you've got me whipped (that, CHUMP is called complacency) and when you let your guard down (start missing meetings) I beat the heck out of you again! How I applaud you and cheer you on each time you get into the fight ring with me again—Hurry, you fool! Love it when you keep coming at me with your right fist cocked; your big punch that you're going to flatten me with. What a laugh! Of course I make sure you don't get wise to the fact that I'm cutting your face to ribbons with my jabs. I let you ignore the blood running down your face from the cuts I've inflicted over your eyes that blind you even further.

I go from grinning, to smirking, to belly-laughing as you stumble around throwing powder puff punches that achieve nothing except to further tire, frustrate, and anger you. Eventually I get quite bored by it all and deck you, and you, you fool, expect me to go to a neutral corner. Hey stupid, I know no honor; I abide by no rules; I am the dirtiest of the street fighters, and I thoroughly, totally, fully enjoy your suffering. How I relish the sight of you, a person of honor, struggling to get to your feet. I stand right next to you and as you get to your knees, I kick you right in the head before you can get to your feet again; (Maybe now you'll understand why relapses are so devastating). I am extremely proficient at map-making. Didn't know that either did you cupcake? I gleefully talk you into using and following MY map!

Oh, to entice you I write on it destinations such as High, Partying, Excitement, etc., etc., etc. In truth they all lead but to one place: And it's not Heaven! You can be very sure, CHUMP, I will do everything possible to camouflage that from you until you have journeyed quite a long and destructive distance with me. How I thrill when I witness clinicians providing their clients with "Tools" to overcome me, and then you meet up with me on the front lines threatening me with your garden trowel. Hey hero don't you see I have a tank and twenty crack ground troops? I will annihilate you, you poor simpleton!

This is a war, not a garden party you are involved in and, something else you apparently don't realize—I do not engage in this war alone! Only a fool would do that (like you do stupid). I, the super strategist, enlist the aid of my allies. The Dealers, the Casinos, Business Deals, Horses? My hired hit men! Your so-called "friends" are actually my "assassins." Mess around with them and they will take you out of play, time after time, after time. I convince you that your hoopla pals in the gin mills and OTB parlors are your true-blue buddies. I sure as hell, make sure you don't listen to the propaganda spoken by the people who care about you—perish the thought! I love to puff you up and feed into that big fat egotistical head of yours, the lie that you are in control—and incredibly you fall for that outright malarkey over, and over, and over again.

Hey gigolo, hey pompous, the moment that you place one bet, CHUMP, one drink, CHUMP, one line CHUMP, one joint, CHUMP, you are a walking time bomb and you're gonna go boom! Heaven forbid you should ever look at your lousy track record for if you ever did it would become exceedingly clear what a swollen-headed prominent, superb ignoramus I am making out of you! Dear me, that does sound a bit sarcastic now doesn't it? Well, you can bet your tush I meant it to be!

Hey c'mon, I always give you what you ask me to—numb out your trouble! You don't really expect me to tell you about the consequences do you? Hey brother, hey sister, what do you expect of me? Surely not to tell you that with each relapse, the price is getting a hell of a lot steeper. That the IOU's are piling up and that each time I numb out what is bothering you, I also automatically numb out your access to your intelligence, your logic, and your upbringing. When you are overcome with remorse, guilt, shame, and anxiety, then you poor fool I tell you my favorite lie. The lie that I can *fix all that* stuff too so you fall for it and drink or gamble some more and the whirlpool of your addiction now progresses ever faster and deeper.

Beginning to get the picture honeybunch? I'm not exactly Mr. Nice Guy or Ms. Friendly! I'll bet you didn't realize that I sit in on every group therapy session, every one-to-one counseling session every AA/NA/GA or GAMANON meeting. How I love the "counselor-pleaser" type, the "clam-upper." I could just kiss the "I don't give a damner," and the "liar" sends chills up and down my spine as I'll be able to grind their faces into the dirt in short order with very little effort needed on my part.

FINAL TIDBITS: I convince you, you are only hurting yourself—and then relish every tortured moment that you dish out to those who love you. I whisper deliciously destructive lies into your ear in a most convincing manner. Lies like "they'll never fire you," and of course I go into ecstasy when I witness the shame for you and your family. It gives me goose bumps when I convince you you'll never be arrested as your future grinds to a halt when you see the flashing lights of a cop's car at your home, or the Feds at the front door! I howl with delight when your bookie or loan shark calls in his bets and you don't have a dime to your name! Just break an arm or slam that hand! Well, Sweetie Pies, I've told you some of my secrets; told you some of my strategies, shared some of my attack plans. Of course, I'm banking on many of you not listening to what I've told you, or thinking it was hogwash and dribble. I intend to capitalize on that and convert you into a CHUMP again—CHUMP!

So long for now, you gorgeous active person you! Of course we shall meet again—and again! I'm looking forward to that! And for those of you in early recovery, Au revoir---certainly not so long, you're doing real good kids!

> *"You have to be tired of the life, because you'll never get tired of the feeling."*
>
> **Edward, addicted to heroin, in recovery**

PCP

"PCP (phencyclidine) was developed in the 1950s as an intravenous anesthetic. Its use in humans was discontinued in 1965, because patients often became agitated, delusional, and irrational while recovering from its anesthetic effects. PCP is illegally manufactured in laboratories and is sold on the street by such names as angel dust, ozone, wack, and rocket fuel. Killer joints and crystal supergrass are names that refer to PCP combined with marijuana. The variety of street names for PCP reflects its bizarre and volatile effects."

"Many PCP abusers are brought to emergency rooms because of PCP overdose or because of the drug's unpleasant psychological effects. In a hospital or detention setting, these people often become violent or suicidal and are very dangerous to themselves and others. They should be kept in a calm setting and not be left alone."

NIDA (NATIONAL INSTITUTE ON DRUG ABUSE)

TRIGGERS

I never realized how truly powerful "triggers" are – those sudden little impulses in our brain that hijack our thinking processes and cause us to make sudden, irrational decisions. For example, a good friend emailed me and before she closed she said she was going to go have some ice cream. Now I had not been thinking of ice cream. It was probably the furthest thing from my mind. In fact, I hadn't even eaten any ice cream in several months, trying very hard to stick with a healthy diet.

Well as Chef Emeril Lagasse says - Bam! The next thing I knew, some unseen and devious forces were taking my hand and leading me to the kitchen, to the freezer, to an orgy of plain vanilla ice cream that had been gathering ice crystals because nobody was eating it; probably because it was plain vanilla ice cream!

That didn't matter though. All I knew was that I wanted that ice cream now and had to have it. Why? Because the trigger had been planted and I couldn't resist it. Well I suppose if I had taken a time out and given myself a good talking to, the desire would have passed. Maybe. Doubtful.

This self-indulgent episode caused me to reflect on what it must be like for a person addicted to drugs or alcohol, and how powerful those triggers must be for them.

On page 156 Dr. Eric Nestler discusses triggers. Read his expert opinion on how to deal with them.

"Scientists are aware that the brain remembers drug triggers. They know that events such as walking through an old neighborhood or hearing a certain song, could lead addicts to relapse. If parts of the brain are still primed to the memories of drug-taking behaviour and have not reset themselves, then it is very difficult to avoid a relapse."
(source - BBC news)

For those of you who are just now experiencing what it's like to live with an addicted person, it's important to remember how powerful triggers are, and see what steps you can take to help the addicted person avoid them, or as Dr. Nestler suggests, "extinguish" them.

More than 60 percent of teens said that drugs were sold, used, or kept at their school.

(www.teendrugabuse.us)

I Am Your Disease
(The Many Faces of Addiction)

Here are excerpts from the 40 compelling, honestly written stories by parents who have lost a child to the disease of addiction. For the full stories you can read them all in I Am Your Disease (The Many Faces of Addiction).

I have edited these excerpts, offering just a glimpse into the lives of these brave moms and dads. The full magnitude of what the parents went through can only be truly appreciated by reading their whole story.

Even these short, edited versions of their stories will sadden you though. They are not included for sensationalism. They are included because we want to open everyone's eyes to see how the disease of addiction shatters lives. We must tell our stories. We are driven to reach out to others. Maybe your child will read this and decide that doing drugs just isn't worth the heartbreak and devastation that they and their families suffer.

These parents poured their hearts out, not so much as a means of healing but rather to help others know that they are not alone in this tremendous battle to slay the Addiction Monster.

As one of the bereaved moms, I found it very difficult to write my son's story in my first book, to expose his life, to put it out there where others might not understand, who might condemn him, not knowing the beautiful, caring person he was. They will see only the disease, the Addiction Monster. But if we are to erase the stigma of a drug-related death, we must speak out in whatever way we can, by whatever means we can. We must let our voices be heard and at the same time let our children's voices be heard. My son had said to me "Mom, nobody wakes up one day and decides to be an addict." Drugs are a choice. Addiction is not.

I didn't find telling Scott's story healing. I truly think only time can help heal us but we'll never be the same and we'll never be completely healed. It's as though a scab has formed over our hearts and we manage to get by, and then something will trigger a beautiful or painful memory and it's as if the scab has been ripped off and we have to begin healing again. Eventually the emotional scar tissue gets thicker and as the years go by, the rip hurts just a little bit less and we grow stronger. Writing our stories opened up a lot of wounds and exposed our underlying heartache laying it bare to be flayed again. If our words help you at all, we are comforted.

"An Angel's Face" By Lucille, Mother of Lenny, Jr.

How do you start a story that changes your life forever?

On July 20, 2003, I got a phone call from my daughter. I'll never forget the words that we exchanged. She said "Ma, I need to talk to dad right away."

I said "Lisa, please don't say it's Lenny."

My precious son had been sitting at his kitchen table for four days. He had overdosed on heroin.

Ms. Heroin wraps her arms around you and doesn't let go. She brings you down evil paths and turns you into a person that you never thought that you could be. And when she lets go it's too late! She turns you into a liar, and a thief and robs all your loved ones.

"My Nine Days of Hell"
By Pam T, Mother of Keith

If there was one message I could give to every parent in America it would be...Never say "Not MY child!"

"Keith OD'd on heroin." The sound, scream, whatever it was that came out of me was so horrible everyone jumped up and our dog hid under the table shaking.

They didn't think he would make it through the night. Not make it through the night???? When I heard those words I felt like my life drained right out of me.

He did live through the night. In fact he lived for nine days!
How in the world do you turn off your child's life support? Yet how in the world do you watch him lie there knowing he would never live a normal life again? Just lie in a coma for as long as he lived."

"Once Upon A Child"
By Sandy, Mother of Jason

Finally, twenty-two hours after his fall I climbed into my son's hospital bed and lay my head on his chest with my arms around him. I placed my ear over his heart so I could listen to the heartbeat. Family and his closest friends surrounded us as the machines were turned off. There was complete silence with the exception of soft sobs that could be heard as people fought back their tears in silence and struggled to maintain composure.

When I was pregnant with Jason, the doctor placed a stethoscope on my tummy. "Would you like to hear your baby's heartbeat?" he asked. I heard the first heartbeats of my child that day. Now, twenty-three years later I lay in a hospital bed with him and once again I listened for his heartbeats. Only this time they were the last...

"MY SON'S JOURNEY TO-WARDS DESTRUCTION"
By Carol, Mother of Mike

It was 7:30 a.m., on a sunny Saturday morning. The phone rang. "Mom? It's Mike, it's bad."

"Call 911, I'll be right there, don't worry he'll be fine."

I ran to the third floor of the apartment they shared, ran in Mike's room...and heard an earth shattering scream come from my mouth. He was cold, very cold, like ice. His eyes were closed, like he was asleep. His upper body and face were purple, he was cold. As I held my youngest son's cold lifeless body in my arms, I saw his cell phone near his right hand, it was open. Was he trying to call me? Oh God, no, God no, please take me and let Mike live.

He was dead. My son was really dead. Words once incomprehensible to me. My world, now shattered, came to a complete and sudden halt. Michael died from a cocaine/heroin overdose at the age of 23.

"I DON'T NEED THERAPY, GOD WILL GET ME THROUGH THIS"

By Maxine, Mother of Lang

One time he told me he needed $40 to get a guy off his back. He said he owed the guy money and the guy had threatened to hurt his sister and/or me if he did not pay him and he had no money. Well, he was so convincing I gave him the $40. Do you know that $40 is what Oxy was going for on the streets? Neither did I. I had given him money to buy a fix.

"My Son's Deadly Choice" By Barbara, Mother of Michael

One day I heard the words that made me collapse and burst into tears. The words that I was told will remain in my head forever. They found my son in a motel room and he was dead.

I am sure that if my son could talk to me, he would say "Mom, the pain and torment that I went through, I hid so well, out of my love for you. As you search for answers and ask all the whys, look up to the Heavens way past the deep blue sky, and remember that you and I had a love for each other that death cannot take away. We will love each other for always. Now I am free at last mom, from this demon called addiction."

"My Beautiful Daughter and Friend" By Sharon, Mother of Samantha

I know there are no guarantees, but in my wildest dreams NEVER, EVER did I think this could happen to us. I would have bet my life. Impossible! Not us! The truth we all now know is it can happen to anyone. Addiction will rip your heart out. No discrimination here. It's an epidemic—in every school, public or private.

It's five dollars for a bag of heroin. It can kill the first time you use it. It's taking our beautiful, brilliant children, our future. It's Satan. It is HELL on earth! IT CAN HAPPEN TO ANYONE! It leaves shattered families and breaks hearts. IT KILLS anyone that gets in its way. Every day another parent will endure the excruciating pain of a knock on the door or phone call informing them that their child's body is in the morgue. You will never be the same, raped of innocence and forever wondering "how could this happen to me?" It can happen to anyone!

"A Life Too Fast"
—By Paul, Father of Josh

I can still feel the hug he gave me two hours before he overdosed. I had gone to see him to congratulate him for being clean a whole year…

Four hours later I got a call from my ex-wife. Josh was being taken to the hospital, and that she had kicked his door down and found him not breathing.

In the hospital, they told me that they thought there was brain damage because they weren't sure how long he had had no air but they were trying to stabilize him.

While all of this was going on his heart started to slow down and I held him as he passed on. My little boy was dead.

"In Loving Memory of Vernon,"
By Jo-Ann, Mother of Vernon

The next morning the police were at my door, telling me that my wonderful son was gone. Now, when it's too late, all his friends feel bad. He is gone. If I had only known he was doing drugs again...The "ifs"...they are tearing me apart.

I have since talked to many of his friends, trying to get them to talk to their parents, to find help. When things like this happen, family and friends are left behind to suffer. Some of them have done so since then, but some are still doing drugs.

"My Precious Johnny Angel," By Grace, Mother of Johnny

My life and my family's life as we knew it was over! I never knew it was possible for a heart to feel such agony and yet continue to beat!

I had many emotions about Johnny's addiction; helplessness, fear, and failure.

I spent many a sleepless night sitting up with Johnny or lying awake, worrying about him. One thing I never felt was shame or embarrassment about my son. He was caught in the grips of his own personal hell.

I miss my son more every day.

Please, if you or someone you love has a substance abuse problem get HELP!

"THE MOMENT MY WORLD CRASHED"

BY JOHNNY'S SISTER, DEBBIE

Saturday, March 18th, 2000, 2:39 AM — The telephone rang. This was not unusual as my husband is a police officer and our phone often rings at night. I had become so accustomed to it that I could answer it in my sleep. But this was different. I don't know why. But for some reason I turned on the light and looked at the clock before answering it. A lady asked to speak to my husband. I knew it was not the police department because they always identify themselves but I did not ask who it was. I think I knew. His words were vague and I sat watching, desperately trying to read his face, fearing the worst possible scenario, that my premonitions had indeed come true. I asked him repeatedly if someone was hurt. He nodded yes. I said "It's Johnny." He again nodded yes. I knew the answer but I asked anyway. "He is dead isn't he?" After what seemed like a lifetime...he slowly nodded...yes.

"SO LITTLE TIME"
By Lisa, Mother of Eddie

I couldn't sleep, I tossed and turned, I conjured up every possible explanation; maybe he lost his phone, maybe the doctor put him in the hospital, maybe he was bingeing, maybe, maybe, maybe but I knew no matter what the situation was, he would find a way to reach somebody.

Unlike so many other diseases that may only affect a certain group of individuals, addiction is a universal, worldwide non-discriminatory disease. It makes no difference where you live, what or whom you know or don't know. Your drug of choice makes no difference either; some people (especially teens and young adults) seem to have the misconception that if they are only taking drugs that a doctor can prescribe, i.e., Xanax, Vicodin, OxyContin, etc., they can't possibly be addicts. This misguided thinking ultimately ended my son's life. Although the Medical Examiner was certain that Eddie overdosed on heroin, had it not been for the alprazolam (Xanax) already in his system, he would have lived.

A Bright Star Now,
By Sandi, Mother of Jennifer

What mother ever thinks that their beautiful 28-year-old daughter would die from a drug overdose?

You watch your child (even at 28 years old, she was my child) and feel helpless. Thus began a spiral downhill. Jennifer was taking methadone, slipping in heroin once in awhile and drinking.

Her last evening was spent drinking and having that one last high on heroin. She didn't plan on dying that night; she just wanted to get high.

The more I reach out to find support from parents like me, the more I learn just how widespread a problem drug addiction is. If telling Jennifer's story can open the eyes of just one teen to its dangers then Jennifer is still here, still that bright shining star.

"THROUGH THE YEARS...WITH MY SON, BRETT, HEAVEN SENT — HEAVEN BOUND" By Chris, Mother of Brett

Soon, I started learning lessons that I never thought I would have to learn. I learned that Xanax and alcohol are a deadly combination that causes severe personality changes.

Wow, how deep in the sand did I have to stick my head to believe that it would not and could not happen to Brett?

He made the decision to try heroin for reasons I will never comprehend. He was desperate...he wanted to start fire school...he wanted his life back. He told his brother **"How did I ever get involved with this and how am I ever going to get out?"** He could not find his way out no matter how hard he tried.

"You're In The Arms Of An Angel" and "Gone But Not Forgotten"

By Lynne, Mother of John and Dennis

Dennis was always so full of life. He was always smiling. I remember about a week before he died, we went out to eat. He kept kissing my cheeks and saying how good he was doing. He was in a half-way house. He seemed so happy.

The next day no one could find him. Then we got a phone call from his best friend. He said they found Denny's van on Kensington Avenue. Someone had OD'd and died. He said he was sure it was Denny.

John was very shy and I believe that's what started his addiction. He went from drinking and smoking pot, to heroin. I remember the last months of John's life. He was finally straight.   was so happy!

He got drunk one day and left.

We looked for him but couldn't find him. I thought he must be in a program. My son was so determined to find John that he called every police station in Philadelphia, and then he called the morgue. They had John. He was found in a vacant lot. He had died of a heroin overdose.

Again I was left to deal with the pain of losing another child. I had not yet come to terms with Dennis's death. Some days I am so overwhelmed with grief. I feel like my heart has been ripped out of my chest.

"I Hope You Have The Time Of Your Life" By Sandi, Mother of Robby

When Robby was 16, he asked me to have a talk with him one night. Since that didn't happen much anymore, I was all ears. Rob began to sob and told me he was addicted to drugs and couldn't stop. I felt like I had been kicked in the gut but tried to remain calm and get more details from him. I asked Robby what kind of drugs he was using and Robby sobbed harder saying it was heroin. Heroin! A death sentence! That's all I could think of. Robby cried that night saying, **"I just want to be a kid again, Mom. I want to stop lying and I want my life back!"**

I had no idea where to turn for help, but promised I would figure it out. Robby wanted to sit up alone in the dark to think. I asked him if this is why he had been sick so often. "Were the drugs making you sick, Rob?"

"Oh my God, Mom! I am sick when I am trying not to use drugs!" and he was.

"Shattered Lives" By Karen, Mother of Gino

He came to us and told us he was addicted to heroin and wanted to go to rehab.

HEROIN???? No one does heroin. Only "street people" do heroin. NOT MY SON!...

Instead of going to his probation meeting, he skipped it and was found dead all alone in a hotel room by himself.

Twelve empty packets of heroin and several needles scattered around and seventy-seven dollars were all they found.

The police were called in and they called the morgue to come get Gino's body.

I wish I could say it ends there but it doesn't. What happened next is what happens all the time in America.

He was taken to the morgue where his body laid for nine days until a funeral home called to ask us what we wanted done with our son's body!

At that point we didn't even know he had died…Can you imagine the shock??

For nine days he laid in a stainless steel drawer, while I paced the floor. Gino's dad spent hours out looking for him in every pawn shop, crack house and abandoned building in Detroit.

They treated him like just another "junkie." Well damn it, this junkie had a family: A family who loved him with all of their hearts:

A family who prayed every night that Gino would get well again.

"The Beginning of a Bad Dream" By Chris, Mother of Ricky

Ricky was in recovery for his addiction for around 3 months. He and his father and brother and sister went out on July 5, 2003, to dirt bike ride in the woods about an hour from home.

Ricky hit a rut in the dirt and the back wheel hit it and flipped him over the handlebars.

My husband took him to the Emergency Room down where they were and he was in so much pain that finally after 5 hours they gave him something. But Ricky explained to the nurse he was a recovering addict and not to give him narcotics for pain. They said ok thank you for letting us know. Ricky also told my husband whose name is Rick also, to make sure the doctors know that he does not want narcotics for pain. That was July 5th, and he was in the hospital until July 9th. He had a broken back and a broken foot. He did fine in the hospital and he looked good other than the pain.

He came home from the hospital at 6:00 p.m. It was a long drive. He had prescriptions and guess what the doctor had prescribed—60 Percocets for the pain! Ricky kept saying he is going to have to go to rehab for pain meds when this was all over.

He overdosed on July 14, 2003. They say it was "benzo," marijuana and heroin.

"Losing Will"
By Rita, Mother of Will

There was a late night knock at the door. I was asleep, but my husband Tim was up. When he heard the knock, he thought that Will must have forgotten his key.

Tim opened the door to find three people in uniform standing on our porch. They asked if this was "the Sommer residence, the home of William Sommer, are you his father, is your wife at home, would you please get her, may we come in to talk to you about William?"

I remember being awoken from a sound sleep. Tim was talking, telling me I had to get up, there were people downstairs who wanted to talk to us about Will.

I remember the somber faces staring at us. I'll never forget the look in their eyes. "We have some bad news," said the one whose uniform was somehow different from the police officers. Her uniform said county coroner. She went on, "Your son was found unresponsive this evening.

We sat. Who were these people? What are they doing in my house? Whatever were they talking about?

They keep talking. We sit, we stare, and we try to understand. We don't move, we can't move.

"Did you know your son was a drug user?"

"We suspect heroin overdose, we'll know more after the autopsy."

They hand us Will's wallet and cell phone. They offer their condolences.

We have just entered hell.

"Mom, Nobody Wakes Up One Day And Decides To Be An Addict" By Sherry, Mother of Scott

"Sherry, answer the phone." Those four, very ordinary words spoken to me by my husband, were the beginning of what would become our nightmarish descent into an existence that we had long feared might happen, but never really believed it would be so...

At Scott's memorial service, his dog Kazak never took her eyes off of Scott's friend on his surfboard. As his friend began to scatter his ashes, suddenly Kazak emitted the most mournful, sorrowful howl that we had ever heard and have not heard since. She knew! Her best buddy was gone, and she knew it.

"I have hurt and shamed myself on numerous occasions although my actions shall not dictate my eternity" By Brigitte, Mother of Jeff

In July an old "friend" who had moved out of the area came to visit. He and Jeff decided to take a ride to see another friend. They made a stop along the way and on Sunday, July 18, 2004, I found Jeff dead in his room—all alone—crumpled in a corner.

I do not wish for any family to have to deal with addiction and I'm really not sure how I got through it, but my love for Jeff kept me going. He hated himself and his life. He hated what this was doing to his family. I tried to understand how this all happened from beginning to end. I have no answers.

"Relax Mom. It ain't that bad. You worry too much." By Margie, Mother of Jim

It was a few weeks, maybe a month after that, that his sister came in the house one evening & told me she hadn`t seen Jim all day & he wouldn`t answer his door, it was locked, and the music was up really loud which wasn`t like Jim to have the music really loud. So I went to check it out. I told my daughter to get me a knife and we`d pry the lock, that maybe he had taken Zeus for a walk.

I pried the lock and the minute I stepped inside I knew he was gone. He looked like he was just sleeping. He`d been gone about 5 hours, or so the coroner said. Everything else after that was just a blur. That`s it, no rehabs, no fights, no jail time. Just gone. The next several days after that were hard, making funeral arrangements. I never had to do this so I was clueless.

"THIS IS BIGGER THAN ME, MOM. IT'S A MONSTER I CAN'T CONTROL"
By Sue, Mother of Katie

I'd been called to the ER by John, my ex-husband, because our daughter, Katie, had been taken there by ambulance. I'd expected an overdose because we'd been struggling to get her in-patient care for her heroin addiction.

Arriving at the hospital, I'd expected her to be admitted for her "qualifying" first overdose for in-patient care. I was puzzled, however, when I was escorted to a closed-door room.

The moment that door opened and I saw John sitting there with a priest, my heart froze. Surely, the situation was grave.

But, that moment lasted only a nano second before John stood up and uttered the words that are indelibly etched into my mind for all eternity: "We lost her."

I've often heard other parents who've lost children tell me that they are having a bad day because it is the anniversary of their child's death, or, it is their child's birthday, or, it is a holiday. I don't have those experiences. I just don't have any special days that are worse than others, because, in my personal grief experience, every day is bad. All of those "special" days don't really stand out for me, because the pain is constant and unrelenting.

"MY GREATEST LOSS," By Michele, Mother of Wade

What people don't understand is the biggest fear we have as bereaved parents is "people will forget our child."

Wade was suffering from mental illness and drug addiction. Dealing with the mental issues was difficult enough, but also dealing with the "monkey on his back called addiction" made survival impossible. Wade would have always struggled in his life, but there was always hope. With the combination of the right people around him he could have had the happy life he had always dreamed of. Drugs made that impossible.

PLEASE, I pray if you are experimenting or thinking about using any type of drugs including marijuana, I beg you, turn your back on them. They will only destroy your life and maybe even cut your life short just like they did for Wade. Life is difficult enough; don't complicate it with drugs because they will eventually destroy you.

I hope that Wade's story has had an impact on your life. There are various degrees of mental illness and drug addictions, but more times than not, the two illnesses are seen together. Drugs lead to an addiction that you don't need. If you are feeling down and depressed, see your doctor and get medical help, please don't start down the path that Wade chose. That path leads nowhere. Without drugs there is always hope, but with drugs, your future is very bleak and dangerous. Don't let what happened to Wade happen to you. Remember, when you are hurting yourself, you are hurting the ones who love you more than you can ever know.

"MY BOBBY,"
By Michele, Mother of Bobby

It was Saturday, July 23rd, 2005, when I heard the horrible news that my Bobby was dead. Bobby had a problem with drugs from the time he was 14 years old, that I knew of. He and I fought the demons for a long time.

Back to that day…I kept calling home, hoping he would answer, hoping he would be making up some excuse why he hadn't been home, but he never did. So I called my answering machine and there was a message from his father…telling me to call him, that it was important! I thought, "Oh God…Bobby got into trouble…maybe locked up, but why would he call his dad?"

I called his dad and my oldest son answered. Bobby sounds just like him, so I said "Bobby where have you been?—I've been worried sick about you." My son Jimmy said, "It's not Bobby mom, it's me Jimmy, here is dad."

His dad got on the phone and told me to get home…BOBBY WAS DEAD! All I remember was screaming---"No! No! No! Not my baby!! You are a liar!"

"A MOTHER'S GREATEST FEAR"
By Kim, Mother of Kara

My daughter Kara died from heart failure 3-4-01 on my living room couch. Kara had been ill for a couple of years, from all her drug use since the age of 12 years old.

Kara was 25 years old when she died. We went through a lot of years of drug abuse with her; dropping out of school 3 months before graduation, running away, and lots more. Before she died she was very much wanting to get off the drugs but did not want to give up most of her friends.

Kara fought hard off and on those months, but could not stay off the drugs. She quit her job in January of 2001, because of her health. She became very weak and had to stay in bed. But on better days, she got up and went out and used.

Parents, do not blame yourself. Our children make their own choices.

"BROKEN DREAMS, LOST PROMISE" By Celeste, Mother of Brandon

I heard that when your child decides to take a drug, that is the last decision they will ever make. The drug makes all the choices after that and I think most families of a lost child will agree that they lost him or her long before their actual death. We tried everything we had to get him back but it wasn't going to happen.

That last day I spoke to Brandon, he was high and we argued as we so often did. My biggest regret is the fights we had. He walked out the door and was gone. Now, looking back, I can't be sure it could have been different but I pray everyday to relieve some of this guilt I carry around and give me my boy back.

The next morning, his friend came to the door and told me she could-n't get him to wake up. We rushed to the hospital, where he lay in a coma due to an overdose of heroin.

We never got a chance to speak to Brandon again or hear him laugh. Dear God, I miss that laugh. Eleven days later we had to say good-bye. The doctors said the brain damage was extensive due to lack of air and he would never breathe on his own again.

"LIVING A PARENT'S WORST NIGHTMARE"
By Phil, Father of Mark

If you were to ask any parent what their biggest fear in life is, their worst nightmare, most would say that it would be losing a child. We are living that nightmare, and it is worse than anyone could have imagined.

The grief due to Mark's death is like no other grief imaginable, however. It is not the normal course of life. Kids shouldn't die before their parents. There are no words to describe the devastation and emptiness. It's not something that you "get over" and the emptiness will always be there.

There seems to be a stigma attached to those who have died a drug related death. Many think that they are bad people who probably deserved their fate. Our son and many other kids who have suffered this fate are caring and wonderful people. Mark gave us so much during his short life and we are so thankful that he is our son. This is not just something that happens to others. This can happen to a friend, a neighbor, or your own child. Sometimes the signs of addiction are obvious, and sometimes they're much more subtle.

"IN A NEW YORK MINUTE, EVERYTHING CAN CHANGE"
By Susan, Mother of Matthew

I lost my son and only child, Matthew on February 11, 2005 to a heroin overdose. He was 21 years old.

I know my son did not want to continue to use drugs, but he was unable to stop. At the time of his death, he had been clean for at least 6 weeks after only one relapse in December. He was going to NA meetings and had just started an outpatient drug program the week before he died. He had never been to rehab. When we asked about it, they told us he didn't do enough! He seemed to be doing very well and I think he convinced himself, as always, that he had it under control. That he could do it "just one more time."

There is a perception that kids use drugs as a way of dealing with pain in their lives and I'm sure that is true for many of them. My son was a very happy person and I think he tried heroin because it was fun and he thought he was invincible. Once he tried heroin, he was unable to stop. He underestimated how dangerous heroin was and he paid for it with his life.

"MY PRECIOUS SON" by Dottie, Mother of Don

One day I had just stepped out on my front porch and a thought came to me that one of my sons was going to die. I thought—which one? But didn't get an answer.

One day in June I had an inclination to pull into a sport store and bought my son an early birthday present, a pair of Nike's and a baseball hat. I'm so glad I did because he never made it to his birthday, which was August 19. I didn't know he would be dead one month later…

He (the cop) came back. He asked if I had a son who was in the Penn Foundation, and he came in and told me that my son, my Don was dead.

I felt like someone had punched me in the stomach. How could that be? He was in such a safe place!

The rest is a blur. He told me to call my husband and to call the Penn Foundation. Oh my God, if I call there, then it must be true. I didn't want to call there. I just kept saying, "NO! NO! NO! I can't do this!"

"FOREVER JUSTIN IN MY HEART" By Linda, Mother of Justin

I could never imagine Justin taking to the dark side of drugs

As a teen he started smoking marijuana. By the age of 20, Justin turned to crack.
In one year he was gone. He spent his 21st birthday in jail and stayed there for four months.

The end of February he came home.

By April 17, 2004, he was gone.

I can't begin to tell you all of the heartache our family is enduring. The loss of my beautiful son left me lifeless. I still cannot believe I will never see that beautiful smile or hear him laugh.

"FOR THE LOVE OF DAVID – OUR BRIGHT AND SHINING STAR" By Kay, Mother of David

January 3, 2000, started like any other day for me.
My husband Al and I ate and then I got ready to go to a meeting. I started down the basement steps to the outside door but something told me to go down and check on David.

I went down a few steps so I could see into his room and there, in the doorway, lay my beautiful son; face up with a rifle on the floor beside him. I ran up the stairs screaming, "Oh, God, he's killed himself."

It had been a suicide, that ugly word that no one wants to speak. Our son had committed suicide and was gone from us forever. We were all crushed and broken and left with so many questions. Why? Was it because of something we did or didn't do? What could we have done to prevent it? God, if you please let us have him back we'll do anything.

" AND I DON'T TAKE DRUGS"
By Jan, Mother of Cindy

Cindy desperately wanted recovery. She was clean and sober several times in recent years, but ultimately fell back into addiction's fatal grasp. This was included in a collection of poetry she wrote while in recovery, during one of many attempts to break free of her addiction. She shared this with me (her mother) when she was drug-free, several months before she died. She was a prolific writer and putting her words down on paper gave her some relief from her struggles.

"UNTIL YOU BEAT THIS THING CALLED ADDICTION, IT WILL DESTROY ALL UNTIL IT IS FICTION"
By Toni, Mother of Ricky

I picked him up at the airport, and for the first time in his life I didn't recognize him when he got off the plane.

I begged and cried and yelled for him to tell me what was wrong with him. He finally started crying and told me he was addicted to heroin. You could have knocked me over with a feather. Not heroin. Not my sweet lovable boy. He would NEVER do that! Well, I moved into action and called all drug information places so I could find out what to do.

We fought and fought. Tried tough love, but I usually gave in. I just loved him so much that I couldn't put him out in his need.

My life ended with his. I am his mother, and I couldn't save him.

Deep down I knew he could die, but never really believed it. Well, believe it! If my son could die, so could anyone else's.

"My Beautiful Son,"
By Barbara, Mother of Joseph

Joe started using weed and some pills in his senior year. He graduated in 2001. Deceased in December, 2002. Heroin took his life and was his drug of choice.

My advice for others who think their kids may be doing drugs would be to find a therapist who has a specialty in addiction treatment. I would also encourage parents of younger teens/teens to read "Yes! Your Kids Are Crazy" and their children should read, "Yes! Your Parents Are Crazy." Both books are written by Dr. Michael Bradley.

"MY PRECIOUS ANGEL JASON"
By Rebie, Mother of Jason

My son Jason died on November 3, 2002, at about 10 a.m., from a drug overdose of heroin and cocaine. He was given a "hot shot" I was told on the back of his neck. He was released from county honor farm in Stockton, at 12 midnight on the 2nd of November 2002, and died the following day, the 3rd .

"DEMONS" BY JASON

Demons all in my head, can't seem to shake them, they're always there. Always watching me, waiting for me. See, there was a time when I was one of them! Doing the things that demons do. Terrorizing my fellow man, why-oh-why I think this way is beyond me. Can't seem to see the light, and find my way. Darkness is most definitely swallowing me.

"MY DAUGHTER, MY BEST FRIEND"
By Madonna, Mother of Shauna

I lost my beautiful daughter Shauna to heroin on August 25, 2005, 12 days after her 20th birthday.

I did all I could to try to help her; counseling, boot camp, psychiatrist, doctors, rehabs, and even jail, but she was not strong enough to fight it.

Shauna was 16, when she first tried heroin in September of 2001, not believing that one time would cause her to be addicted for life.

You all know how the story ends… "the phone call," the drive to the hospital. Only in my case I did not know her condition. I thought it was a trip to pick her up after she overdid it…yet again…

"My Honey Boy" By Ann,
Mother of David

My son, my Honey Boy as I always called him, David Hall, of Kokomo, Indiana, went to be with the Lord on July 3, 2001. He was just 23 years old.
I can still hear the words from his dad on the phone. He was crying and I KNEW something bad had happened. Never did I dream it was David.
I had just talked to David the night before. We talked almost every day. He sometimes would get upset because I called so much, but after all, I'm a Mom.

It still seems like yesterday.

I still want to tell the world! I had business cards made that have David's picture and information about his passing on them. I give them to everyone I can. I want everyone to know it CAN happen to them.

Drugs don't care if you're poor or rich, what color you are, where you live, how smart you are, what kind of person you are, what church you belong to or don't belong to, if you have a family who loves you or you're just living on the streets.

"Ignorant Of The Truth" By Pam M, Mother of Keith

In the early hours of November 14th, 2004, my husband, Bill and I received a knock at our door. This was the kind of knock that every parent fears but, in their heart, never really thinks will happen to them. The officer told us that our 19 year old son, Keith, had died, but that he did not have any details. We were forced to wait some 20 minutes until the coroner called us with more information.

Within those 20 minutes, Bill and I speculated as to what might have happened. We had agreed that a car accident was the most obvious thing we could think of.

What the coroner finally told us tilted our world. Keith had died of a drug overdose. "This couldn't be," we thought. "Our son doesn't do hard drugs."

As with other things I do now, I write this story in hopes that other parents wake up to the fact that even the "boy next door" can get themselves into the world of drugs.

"YOU ARE SO BEAUTIFUL TO ME," By Robin, Mother of Sara

"You are so beautiful to me." That was my song to her ever since she was born. The day before she died, I picked her up at my sister's and she said "Hey Mom, I have a surprise for you." She took my hand, brought me into the living room, went to the stereo, turned on a CD that she had made by downloading music, skipped a few songs, then

Joe Cocker comes on and she took my hand and we danced to the song holding each other very close. Eighteen hours later, she was gone.

I wish I could say that it was one of her "bad choice" friends that gave her the drugs that cost her, her life, but I can't. The drugs were my brother-in-law's. She spent the night at my sister's house and got hold of my brother-in-law's Methadone. From what I have been told, she was watching a movie, fell asleep on the couch, and never woke up.

Author's Note: These are just parts of heart-wrenching stories by 40 parents. There are thousands more of these stories taking place throughout the year. If we all speak up about addiction, and write our representatives and campaign for free, long term rehabs, perhaps we can get our children the help they deserve.

While it's too late for the children in this book, it doesn't have to be too late for others. Every voice speaking out, every letter written, every telephone call, every email to our representatives, every protest, may eventually bring much needed reform. We have to try...for them and all the others who will follow.

"They can because they think they can"

Virgil, Classical Roman Poet

AFTERWORD

This has been a difficult and arduous book to write. This is not a subject that anyone wants to think about, or to dwell on. It is especially not something that anyone wants to have lived through.

The people in this book have lived through hell, some for longer periods than others. They offer advice for other people who are now living this nightmare, not because they are experts, but because they need to reach out to help others. By helping others, they themselves are helped.

As in my first book, I do not speak for everyone in this book. They have spoken so beautifully themselves and have given loving advice. They have not pulled any punches. They've spoken directly and honestly from the heart.

Anyone who has lived with an addicted person knows what fear is. The fear that each new day may be The One…the day that we receive that call or knock on the door. Anyone who has lived with that fear only to have that deepest fear realized, now must spend the rest of their lives trying to pick up the shattered pieces and fashion a new life together out of the shards. The pieces will be reassembled, but the cracks and fissures remain.

Some will gain new strength and the cracks will not be as noticeable. Others may never get those pieces back together again. We are all different. We all grieve differently. There is no right or wrong way to grieve. There is also no time limit on grief. It remains as does the love for our lost loved one.

I hope this book has helped you understand more about the disease of addiction. There is so much we've all learned since we lost our child. We'll never know if we could have saved our child with this new knowledge. But perhaps it can help you.

Our children made a mistake in their youth. Unlike other youthful indiscretions, the choice to do that first drug proved to be a deadly choice. They did not choose addiction.

This book was written in honor of everyone who has struggled with this disease. It is also written in honor of the people who have wisely chosen not to do drugs. It is especially written in honor of all the parents and grandparents and siblings and friends who helplessly watched as their loved ones descended into the maelstrom of drugs, unable to help them.

If you want to do something to help addicted people, I urge you to contact your state representatives and implore them to stop incarcerating nonviolent drug users and instead spend our tax dollars on free, long term rehabs where addicted people will get treatment. It's the humane thing to do.

Websites and online support groups

Angels of Addiction (www.angelsofaddiction@yahoo groups.com)

RememberMeInHeaven@yahoogroups.com

RememberedInHeaven@yahoogroups.com

www. HARMD.org

www. MAMA.org

www. familieschangingamerica.org

www. thewrongpathtaken.com

www. dyingtogethigh.com

www. phoenixpsychotherapy.com

www. iamyourdisease.com – (author's website and email address)

www. opiaterecovery.com

www. heriticsofheroin@ groups.msn.com

www. ourwall.net

Sheryl Letzgus McGinnis is the author of I Am Your Disease (The Many Faces of Addiction, her first book, written after the tragic death of her youngest son, Scott Graeme McGinnis, RN from a drug overdose.

Sheryl has been interviewed on radio stations, satellite radio, and TV. She has spoken at her local library on drug addiction and has several speaking engagements coming up in the fall of 2008. She is an Expert Platinum Author on the internet site www. Ezine.com and writes many articles on addiction and has also been a featured Op-Ed writer for a Mother's Day piece in the *Florida Times Union*.

Slaying the Addiction Monster is her second book. Simultaneously while writing this book, she also wrote a book for middle school children called The Addiction Monster and the Square Cat.

The Addiction Monster and the Square Cat is a fictionalized version of her son Scott's descent into the world of drugs, his long struggle to overcome the addiction and to slay the monster, as told by a very sassy but likable cat named Pumpkin. Pumpkin implores children not to do drugs and speaks to them in a humorous way. The story is not only about Scott but about other children who have died from drugs because they didn't believe a person could become addicted after trying drugs only one time. This book is aimed specifically at children in the 5th and 6th grades and up. Sadly, the age of children who try drugs is getting younger and younger. Sheryl believes that education will be our salvation and she is passionate about educating children to the dangers of drugs.

Sheryl is married to retired science teacher, Jack McGinnis. Their son Dale, lives near by and is a full time grad student. The McGinnises are owned by 1 beautiful lab, (their son Scott's dog,) and 4 spoiled cats. They live in Palm Bay, Florida. Sheryl is always available to speak about addiction. She is on the Parent Advisory Board of the Partnership For a Drug-Free America.

35203373R00167